DEATH BEYOND THE JADE GATE

Melike

First paperback edition: June 2023

Cover design by Bella. Created with Microsoft Designer.

ISBN-13: 9798399641300 (paperback)

Published by Melike

This book is dedicated to those Uyghur heroes the world is just getting to know.

CONTENTS

PREFACE

Most of the books I read was between the age of eleven and twenty-one years old. It was 1966 to 1976, the time of the Great Cultural Revolution in China. Even a cultural one, revolution is certainly not a gala dinner. It was more like an educational extermination, borne out of power struggles, nothing to do with hope and future. With education put on hold, I would play hopscotch in the street with my friends during the day and had fun with the books I could get my hands on in the evening. Public libraries were a rare thing in China during those days, at least not at primary school level. I usually borrowed the books I saw other people were reading, like asking my friend's father to lend me the book he was clearly enjoying. It was written by the Chinese literature giant Lu Xun; that was how I finally got to know the writer and became a fan of his. However, a story I read then intrigued me a lot and took me decades to decipher.

A whole household was delighted when a son was

born. During a gathering the one-month-old baby was carried out to the guests (until that day babies were usually kept away from outside world for their safety). The purpose for this was to satisfy the crowd's curiosity and to be complimented at the same time in local tradition. As usual the one who said the child would become rich one day was heartily thanked; another one who predicted a famous future for the baby was also praised for his insight in return. Then came the unorthodox comment which shocked the host and guests in the same manner. 'The child will die' was the realistic prediction, then the person who spoke so honestly (and harshly by my opinion) was thoroughly beaten by the family.

With this tale, Lu Xun condemned the tremendous reward for telling lies and the punishment followed by revealing the truth. I didn't understand the concept then, for me the prediction of death sounded like the curse from the witch in Sleeping Beauty with bad luck to follow. Or like announcing the world is nothing more than a boneyard without acknowledging the sunny glitter that appeared with the arrival of the new life. Should people be allowed to talk about death to a newborn baby? A baby who has many tomorrows to greet, many wishes to fulfil before encountering that inevitable death in a very distant future.

Not that I had never heard of death then. I wasn't even five years old when my big sister told me about her classmate Pan Huijun, who was dying from an incurable disease. Now looking back, I think it might be acute leukemia. Pan was the prettiest and cleverest girl out of fifty pupils in her class, the teacher's pet, but had to attend hospital instead of her school for medical treatment. She was brought back to school for one last time to say goodbye to everyone with a shaven head, as the cruel medical intervention had already claimed her pretty curly locks. A few days later the teacher informed the class about Pan's death. Apparently the teacher sobbed uncontrollably, and I cried my eyes out at home with my big sister.

A few years later, my sister, with her story-telling hobby, revealed to us that her classmate's Japanese mother was dying of a fatal disease (must be cancer in an era with many mysterious illnesses yet to be named). There was a twist in the tragedy, since the sickly woman was advised to drink turtle blood to rid the demise, but she refused and died. I spent years feeling sad that she chose to die rather than to live, until I was old enough to understand not all illnesses have a cure and turtle blood is no medicine. It was just another Chinese fancy drug with over-hyped miracle cure power because of its scarce nature. Mother told me that it is not possible for the Japanese to try this type of odd treatment while the Han Chinese willingly do.

At that age death still felt like it belonged to unfortunate ones only, but all that has changed since I entered my seventh decade in life. It must have taken half a century for me to come anywhere near to Lu Xun's wisdom, sadly only after many of my beloved ones have all departed. So far I have lost my parents, my brother, my husband and many more friends and relatives. Looking back at their lives, some were more accomplished than others, yet none of them was remotely rich or famous. So death is the hard reality of life while money and fame are mere fantasies most of us are sucked into. Such is the peril of life.

A word as powerful as death raises fear and brings back unpleasant memories, hence the physical punishment in the gathering of Lu Xun's tale. We mourn privately, like my constantly visiting that earth-shattering moment when death came to take my cancer-stricken husband away. My sky ceased to be blue and under the dusky cloud I can only feel half-alive. Being a medical doctor for 49 years seemed not long enough for my husband to greet death with glee. He gracefully or dutifully iterated the message that everyone dies. Sadly, not even a gleam could be found in his static stare. Gone was the flame from his fiery gaze which was usually the reflection of his passion for life.

Consciousness of mortality only became part of my life after half of my heart was ripped out and buried next to my loved ones. This is the death that Lu Xun talked about to heighten the awareness of our existence on earth. He knew we would start talking about our destiny sooner or later.

CHAPTER 1 FATHER

If death is nothing at all, we will be enjoying summer and fall; we shall talk and laugh as we have always done, instead of waiting for my time to come.

Father was born the year before The First World War to a wealthy Uyghur family in Atush, a Central Asian province near Kashgar. Life immediately unfolded itself to him in an unfavourable way: at the age of four he saw his family fortune decline with the arrival of the October Revolution. At only sixteen years old, he lost his mother to tuberculosis. In his early twenties, when he was trying to help Uyghur children to get a grip of education, his nationalist teacher Memtili Efendi was jailed by the Sheng Shicai's Government[1]. Father was also on the blacklist as the personal assistant to the educator, but managed to escape in time to not be crucified as well. The prison fire in Kashgar which burnt his mentor and three hundred inmates to ashes must have wounded Father's sorrowful heart to never heal and forever bled with flashbacks.

The tragedy forced Father to practice acceptance as he helplessly watched the short-lived Second Eastern Turkestan Republic being crushed and our president, Ehmatjan Qasimi, perished in a mysterious plane crash with all his colleagues. The grip of nightmare continued when the Chinese People's Liberation Army marched into Xinjiang and threw Father into jail for crimes he never committed. As the situation grew more severe, no one would dare to be a businessman anymore, Father found his way to Harbin in 1958. With his spirits crushed and fragments of them scattered all over his birthplace, he started rebuilding his life three thousand miles away. The dairy farm he owned for the next 25 years gave him tremendous solace. In a time when most people in China were still starving, he was able to provide us a life of plentiful food plus clothes in a spacious house with a tree garden. At the age of 91 he died peacefully in Urumqi, at his sanctified home of the Uyghur city. It was December 2004, three weeks before the unprecedented tsunami devastated the world.

Father was one of the thirteen children my grandmother gave birth to in her short forty years of life, and she lost eight of them very soon. It must have been common to have such a high infant mortality in Central Asia at that time, since Mother was also one of the five survivors out of thirteen siblings. Apart from succumbing to common childhood diseases like measles, many infants also died from the symptoms of a less threatening nature, like diarrhea. Fat was treated as a precious drug by medically ignorant local people. Instead of limiting the ailing children's diet to plain bread and rice, more milk and butter contaminated the infants' intestines further to bring them to their deathbed. Both of my parents lived to the age of 91, so the weaker peers were wiped out long before they could even taste the fruit of life.

My grandfather, who kept all his savings in Russian Rouble like other Uyghurs at that time, saw the chest full of his money turned into useless paper overnight. I assume trading with our Russian Central Asian cousins must be the need for the currency, but the October Revolution brought in the communist regime with a new currency. The received wisdom enabled Uyghurs to invest their savings in gold coins rather than any form of currency hereafter. My grandfather remained the richest man in the village, but with a lot less money to spend.

Father was educated in Madras, that explains his staunch religious belief, something he tried to impose on all his daughters unsuccessfully. Madras might not be an enlightenment-spreading or wit-kindling school, but it was the only place for young boys and girls to learn to read and write then (yes, my aunts went along to Madras with my father and uncle). Much to my surprise years later in Harbin, the Han Chinese always admired my grandparents and even my parents' literary skill. In school I was taught how illiterate the Han Chinese were until universal education was made available after the arrival of the communist regime in 1949. No wonder the Han Chinese ladies called Lady McCarthy a literary great in *An English Lady in Chinese Turkestan*, when they realised she was not just scribbling for fun but writing real letters home to her mother in England. All to her amusement.

The dull bit of studying in Madras was that you were asked only to read the Koran for the rest of your life to rejuvenate your faith. I was among the generation also restricted to read one book only during the Cultural Revolution years, and was utterly bored of the Chairman Mao's works. Seeing all other books were banned or burned for their supposedly allegorical content, I dreamt for the day to be freed to delve into those stories. The pleasure of being curious at the beginning, informed in the middle and satisfied at the end can't be obtained from one book only. Mother, who was always quick in drawing conclusions, (with some ludicrous ones like eating chicken gives you darker hair) did for once correctly point out the similarities between communism and Islam. Actually she put it more bluntly than me, according to her Chairman Mao learnt his trade from Prophet Muhammad to stay saint for thousand years to come.

The other benefit for being Muslim is going on a pilgrimage, to set foot outside from your immediate world and bring back fresh ideas to ignite the lows of the static local life. Some Uyghur pilgrims admired the way children went to school in Balkans and came back to start opening real schools besides Madras to spread scientific knowledge. A spectacular achievement always blocked by the Chinese government, applied specifically with a policy to bound Uyghurs in a barbaric mould with no opportunity to be acquisitive to knowledge. One governor of Xinjiang boasted about his successful reign there while claiming he achieved that through giving us Uyghurs what we wanted. "What if they want your power?" asked Dowager Xi, the empress of that era. His answer was that there was no chance for it to happen, since he made sure Uyghurs remained ignorantly uneducated and would never crave freedom, justice or power.

More than a century ago, on horseback only, Uyghurs had to spend an entire year for a round trip from Central Asia to Mecca. To cover the extraneous expense of the journey and support the family left behind, pilgrims carried goods sold well in Arabic land and brought back new products for local Uyghurs' need. One might argue that Uyghurs are not serious Muslims to mix business with religion, but it certainly made Hajj a more attractive voyage. As we are people living in the land most remote from the pelagic zone, to have a glimpse of the vast sea, to cross multiple countries en route must have felt like flying through outer space for that era. Both of my grandfathers completed their Hajj performance during the early 1920s. With financial bonus, of course. They survived the harsh journey in the scorching heat, not to mention the shivery cold to tell their amazing peregrination. They were crowned with the title *Aji* in our traditional bearing. A well-deserved honour.

The risky trek in the wilderness was not without its tragic endings too. Mother's uncle was never to return from his highly anticipated journey. His companions diminishingly wrote him off as lost during the arduous expedition. My inconsolable grandmother never completely got over her brother's untimely death. Actually murder, as she claimed. He was a quick-tempered landowner, who might have offended people he should never have went to Hajj with. The culprits on the other hand got away with all murders, since the chance to unearth the evidence in the endless ragged barren field is like looking for a needle in a haystack. The hazardous route to Hajj which was renowned once as the Silk Road must be littered with Uyghur bones and haunted shallow graves. There were also bodies of the perished weak and old pilgrims, who inevitably passed away from their illness.

Pilgrimage is the source of some bizarre anecdotes too: an Uyghur pilgrim stopped to pray in an Egyptian mosque vociferously one afternoon. Nearby an overworked native woman was spinning cotton balls into yarn. She was annoyed with the incessant disruption from her young son. Furiously the woman put a spell on her son, to be turned into that poorly praying Uyghur pilgrim for eternity. Unbeknownst to her that he was a wealthy, esteemed Uyghur Islamic scholar. The man virtually knew the entire Koran by heart and was admired by his countrymen whenever he vocalized the Ayet (verse from Koran). However, to recite the Koran with an Uyghur accent must be so abhorrent even to an untrained Arabic ear.

By the time Father could complete his lifetime ambition to go on the pilgrimage, he was already 73 years old. There was still no diplomatic relationship between China and Saudi Arabia then. The millennials might find it strange that the communist China was the Taliban equivalent of 1950 and 1960. At least it took Saudi Arabia 41 years to give up Taiwan and accept the People's Republic as the legitimate country for Chinese people. Father had to go to a third country to apply for a visa for his Hajj journey. Actually there was even a fourth country, Iraq, in his trip. After he traveled by plane to Turkiye to obtain his visa, Father then took a coach to Mecca with Mother.

It was 1986, I was quite concerned seeing them going through Iraq while the war was still raging on with Iran. Surprisingly not a gunshot was heard - instead my parents only gushed about the beauty of Iraq as a country, with orderly rows of grape vines lined up all the way. At night time they slept under the stars and got up in the morning to continue their journey, then reached Mecca in three days. It is hard to imagine anyone would dare to attempt the same journey through violence-riddled Iraq today. The passengers would either be pulled out from their coach to be shot or slaughtered during their open air rest at night. Initially I was unhappy that they didn't take the easy route to travel by air, but their first hand information from their six days trip (three more days for return) on the road delighted me later. A country we all only saw on TV before became vividly alive.

Father never missed a single prayer, which was quite an achievement when almost all mosques were desecrated in his lifetime. With his talent in singing, his melodic chant of Koran was a musical treat to the ear. I used to wake up at dawn to the rhythms and cadence of his first prayer. The rest he prayed after darkness descended. One of his solitary evenings was interrupted by my brother's Han Chinese colleague, who was perplexed to see Father standing there facing the wall (Mecca actually). He dashed out to ask why Father was impervious to his greeting. My quick-witted mother told him that Father was dealing with the upset which my brother caused earlier. 'What a spooky temper!' he exclaimed. He didn't stop there, since that day he would constantly advise my brother to never disobey Father again. "Don't make the old man stare at the wall in the darkness alone", he warned repeatedly

Prayer was introduced to Muslim men as a means to dispense moral lesson rather than meditation. It did make sense in an era of no TV, no internet, not even many books to keep people occupied. What can be worse than seeing men somewhat indulge in roving eyes away from God? The solution was for men to pray over 30 times a day, to remain attached to Allah while detached to their environment. However, it proved problematic to pray all day once the ancient life of simplicity gave way to modern sophistication. This resulted in the prayers being reduced to a reasonable five times a day. People need not take the trouble to implore the divine all day long at the cost of ignoring their earthly duty. Whereas Shias have settled to a more sensible three times daily routine.

Father was unique, since most Uyghurs only pray during Eid. The few who pray daily usually do it once in the morning. Others embraced a fairer solution: to complete all five prayers as a half hour assignment in the realm of night. To survive with Islamic beliefs under communist restrictions is what we Central Asians have excelled in. Despite the immense oppression, we have effectively managed to integrate Islam into our culture seamlessly. Even the Chinese government was unable to work out where our culture starts and religion ends. It is a mystic Islam we have embraced, with a vastly more complex cosmic origin. We are still fascinated with the sky, sun, stars and celebrate Nowruz. Something in our culture cries for wisdom, healing and resistances to ominous Chinese assimilation.

A fellow student tried to convince me to embrace Christianity when I was in university during the early 1980s. He was baptized and proudly showed off his photos from church and pool. With limited interest in religion, I was hard to impress. However to his hunting eyes my jeans, t-shirts and short skirts were not Muslim-like, as a result he expected me to take the leap of faith without a hitch. Only when I turned down his invitation to Billy Graham's rally, he saw all wasn't going swimmingly. Little did he know that all Uyghurs are born Muslims and we don't regard Arabic fashion as Islamic costume. Besides, under the bleak reality where communism rules, one has to formulate a strategy not to go astray from the narrowly-defined freedom of expression. An outward Muslim lookalike appearance has its consequences - harbouring a secret faith in our heart is the only safe option. My personal take on Islam is: never consume pork products and always celebrate Eid.

Even Eid can be celebrated like a cultural event when religious festivals were disallowed. For two days a year we join Muslims in different corners of the world to observe Eid quietly, then we will commemorate our loved ones befittingly, especially those who could join us no more. A single Uyghur family in Harbin, ours was a tiny community made up of only six family members. Father would pray for cosmic bliss to behold the heavenly light on my grandparents forever, also for the rest of the faded crowd from spirit to spirit. As children we craved luscious food, modish clothes and dancing to Uyghur folk music. No TV, no internet, not even a telephone to converse, but we felt connected beyond the spatial realm with other Muslims on our planet. Those clandestine Eid celebrations are worth reminiscing for.

Religion has become essential for humans to deal with our reluctance to accept our temporary existence in a world we don't fully understand.

It is also the only way to deal with concepts like souls and consciousness so far. The eternity Buddhism introduced has been music to our ears, which has left everyone competing for the dews of heaven ever since. What always amazes me is the simplicity of heaven and the complexity of hell, distinctively sophisticated. The eerie Chinese hell is aptly named *underground prison* with chaotic, intricate eighteen levels of maze. By contrast the celestial hierarchy is only nine-fold. The treacherous and maddening purpose of hell is designated to perform the supposedly fair but seemingly gruesome ways of torture. The dispatched message is loud and clear: behave as you are told during your short journey on earth to qualify for a happily ever after existence in a celestial blue world.

The other religions have been unable to come up with anything more original, just dutifully echoing the scary fact of the hell which we will endure hereafter. There is no preaching of character building, no advice on necessity to accept responsibly during our one and only significant life on earth. The core doctrine of theology remains to be that two imaginary birds in the bush are better than a real one in the hand. With so many tangled roots, why anyone would try to convert others to join their own faith is a myth to me. Someone apparently did succeed in convincing a Tibetan to swap Dalai Lama with

Jesus Christ. I doubt the Bible can be as useful as the age-old Tibetan aphorism and folklore. To survive in the breathtakingly beautiful yet challenging Tibetan Plateau, one needs traditional wisdom.

Some people seem guaranteed a place in paradise, such as Uyghur men with more than seven daughters, since his life in this world will be surely torturous as hell already. Instead of questioning why Islam is hard on women, Father was determined to save us, his three daughters from being condemned to the abyss by enabling our prayers reaching to the clouds. He tried hard to keep us pious and straight, while authorities preached atheism in school. Father gained the upper hand when the two worlds collided around us. He planted the fear of God in our heads. The grave peril lingered in my life for so long; rather than having fun during my teenage years I was fixated on afterlife and the unloving God.

With such obsession I even searched for books to get a glimpse of the impending apocalypse. It was not Armageddon that I found, since no one could get hold of a Bible during the Cultural Revolution. However the Chinese books filled with the horrifying pictures of *Diyu* had always been at hand. The *underground prison* maze torturing wronged souls is a visual calamity that can make anyone anxious and not worth the labour for reading according to my teacher.

My newly found knowledge of religious punishment did make my curious father sit down with me and look through the illustrations. He then showed his appreciation to why Islam forbids graphic representations. 'Nothing here is heavenly, and the hell is the replica of the sadistic activities from the criminal underworld on *Red Dust*', he said. As usual, Father impressed me with his constant learning by using Chinese words *Red Dust* to describe our earthly life here. I didn't challenge him for sounding like our teacher, who claimed humans created God from our own image. I wanted to please Father by keeping Islam near and dear to my heart if only he could assure me that Islam treats sinners a bit kinder.

It was in the early 1970s the Chinese government started promoting cremation due to the shortage of burial land. The new concept, though sadly death-related, became a dinner table topic and came with its own jokes too. Witnessing people willingly being burnt as soon as they were dead, made me rethink the true nature of the judgement day finale. It became obvious that the cremation wasn't painful, rather a more assuredly calm and swift process. All this evidence was sufficient to put my mind at ease, and I was finally able to get on with my one and truly existing life without fear. Gradually even God appeared less needy and more passionate to me. What to worry when day regularly comes after night, summer is never skipped before the arrival of winter? Needless to say that no one is looking forward to the arrival of eternity. Thank God it is in a distant future, at a far away land, in an oblivious world and at an old age for most of us.

While my logic was helping me to become the person I strive to be, Father was at pain to bolster my innermost fear which can drive me back to God. For Father life is sad and chaotic, religion is the instructions to the soul that can lead us to our already mapped out destiny. Asking Father why we are even given a brain wouldn't shatter his illusion. He need not invent new stories for appeal, since he was a firm believer that we never had much brain to start with, until Eve, mother of the human race tasted the forbidden fruit and forever spoiled our blissful ignorance. He could go to great lengths to express his biblical-inspired thoughts and make me wonder if Father ever practiced what he had just preached: to submit himself to the divine hand who created him.

Father was an accomplished singer, he accompanied himself on the delightful effect from the duttar, the most popular Uyghur two-stringed musical instrument when he sang. For Mother his best musical acts were those performed by Father's younger self on his rooftop. It might sound crazy, but we Central Asians have been living in bungalows with flat roofs for centuries because of our arid climate. I have seen young Uyghur men charmingly singing and playing the duttar on the rooftop in films, no less glorious than any bona fide stage performance. In the early 1980s one of Father's home-made cassettes became very popular in Ghulja. There was even a story circulated with his Uyghur folk songs together: unhappy with the style of the pop songs from that time, he recorded his own music in traditional style to show the Uyghur youth how it should be done. In small ways Father probably did feel compelled to tell young people not to go astray from our already endangered culture, but to see him accepted as a dynamically functioning musician was a pleasant surprise to us.

The first time I saw a duttar was in 1973 when my brother brought one back from his trip to Urumqi. Despite its exquisitely defined form, the head of duttar was generally rather large and fragile, made from hollowed-out mulberry wood. How did my brother manage to hold onto it on a week-long journey on an often crowded train? It was astounding to see he brought the pristine instrument back without a crack which wasn't equipped with a protective case either. Then the fascinating time for listening to beautiful Uyghur folk songs started and Father sang them with true emotions. The songs often told stories of young men and even women on horseback who sacrificed their lives for freedom and justice. I still have so many lovely memories of those cold Harbin winter nights, the whole family gathered around the stove with scattered orange peel to enjoy Father's singing. The aromatic orange scent still brings those amazing home concerts back to me now.

The power of haunting lyrics continuously enables Father's most cherished song to reverberate in my head without break. How can our homeland be cleansed with our ancestors' blood! Despite the metaphor here being about the cruel nature of fought war, it would be weeping tears rather than the divine blood I prefer. Then we are told to take pride as Genghis Khan's descendants. Isn't Genghis Khan Mongol? Father said he was one of us while a Kazakh friend insisted Genghis Khan had a Kazakh mother. I was still hesitant to claim Genghis Khan as our own, until a few years ago I found out that Korea claims that he is Korean, while Russians maintain that Genghis Khan is one of them. At least my Uyghur ancestors followed Genghis Khan to the West to fight the battles, so were part of his successful world domination. I am finally able to sing the song proudly to commemorate Memtili Efendi, as Father told me it was his mentor who composed this beautiful melody with optimism behind its irrefutable melancholy.

As a trailblazing teacher, Memtili Efendi brought back the idea that knowledge is power from The West. Father became his most ardent student and ditched his long Central Asian shirt for Western-style suits I saw him wearing all his life. Father eagerly joined his mentor in educating young Uyghur children to unlock their full potential, that subsequently ignited a life-long learning and teaching passion in Father. Memtili Efendi played the tembor (a five metal stringed musical instrument) while Father played his duttar; together they taught children to sing the nationalistic songs. They spent all their days to help the children develop their language and mathematical skills and Father was nicknamed Zeki for his diligence and inimitable energy.

Nonetheless, the uplift education can bring to the society is a forbidden fruit for non-Han Chinese ethnic groups. In 1937, the ruthless Chinese Nationalist Government closed the schools and murdered Memtili Efendi, the supreme Uyghur educator, for his enlightenment movement in Kashgar. Being his teacher's most trusted confidante and personal assistant was a punishable offence, as a result Father had to make a swift escape to Khotan just before the soldiers were dispatched to arrest him. Father became a businessman following the ineluctable family tradition. He made a success of his business while remaining attached to his books and music.

During the mid-1950s Father was offered a job to work in the educational department of Xinjiang by Saifuddin Azizi, the top governor of Xinjiang Autonomous Region. Saifuddin Azizi was Father's one-time classmate and the nephew of their beloved and revered heroic teacher. Disheartened by communism, Father declined the offer. He educated us, his four children instead, with great satisfaction. Even at the bleak time for education during the Cultural Revolution, he wasn't daunted by the burnt books or exiled intellectuals. He was able to finance us to be privately educated by our Russian teacher in Harbin. I always felt it was a tragic loss for the Uyghur nation not to have him to be the public educator for their children. There must be many restrictions set up by the Chinese authorities; still one can get round and elicit talents among the Uyghur youth. I sensed some sort of regret from Father later in his life, with unfulfilled desire of his own Father encouraged us to become university lecturers in Xinjiang once we gained our university degrees.

Having survived the imminent arrest and execution himself, Father advised us to keep out of politics, which he described as a fire that burnt all those who touch it. I wasn't even allowed to mention our independence when I was young enough to believe it would sort out all our problems. Father also despised communism, since the Nationalist Chinese Government, who committed mass murder in Xinjiang, was under the spell of Stalin from the Soviet Union then. He also witnessed the effect of famine during the 1920s through the hungry Russian soldiers at our border. Desperate for a slice of bread, the starved Russian border guards were willing to give away their stylish military uniform, then would swallow the bread in a gulp hungrily. It was little wonder that Father didn't take up the opportunity to study in Tashkent like his contemporaries, it enabled him to examine all aspects of Bolshevik more clearly as an outsider. His definition of communism was their ability to suppress productivity. The market, according to Father was full of goods for traders to shift, and became empty with the arrival of communism. Suddenly there was even famine.

Father was not a simpleton Muslim, as a talented singer he turned reciting the Koran into a musical treat for us. Even now I wince when I hear imams reciting Ayet tunelessly, as compared to Father's musical interpretation. Besides, his enduring faith was unmistakably multilayered. He was an enthusiastic admirer of the Dalai Lama; he saw good in every religion in the world and always claimed that we all share the same God. He didn't even bother to answer my questions about the Sunni and Shia differences, since he advocated the oneness of religion, how could he divide Muslims who all are prophet Muhammad's followers! I know that he agreed with Dalai Lama's saying that the only true religion consists of having a good heart, but for him to extend it to say religious people are all good is certainly a misconception. For me being religious is no more than a hobby or pastime. It is like those joining the gym for a healthy body or simple satisfaction. Very often the ones who spend hours in the gym every day are never as healthy as people who embark an active life and ditch junk food at the same time.

Father wasn't the only person linking religion to good behaviour. When I was growing up in China, there were always whispers about how kind Catholic Christians are. The Chinese Catholics are descendants of people who were converted by Christian missionaries during the 19th century. Unfortunately most of them even had to hide their belief during the Cultural Revolution. Call them victims if you like, but how could they all be wonderful human beings! After the invasion of Iraq, one of my supposedly sensible neighbours expressed her profound disdain to see Tony Blair starting a war while being Catholic. In her wayward reality she confused our then prime minister with his unelected Catholic wife, and conveniently forgot that the Spanish Armada escorted an army to invade England during Queen Elizabeth I's time! Agitated with my facts she disengaged herself from our conversation with her usual charming smile save that of gritting teeth.

Back to Father, he was kind by heart and enjoyed helping people throughout his life. He always felt sorry for those who were less fortunate than us. During the famine in early 1960s, he offered a Han Chinese he never met before ten kilograms of rice. To give away our barely enough ration then buy the rice from the black market with more than twice the official price was a huge sacrifice. It didn't worry Father, since the man's story that his children were starving at home saddened him so much, for a few days Father claimed he couldn't get the image of hungry crying children out of his head. We never saw the man again, but prayed that he and his children got through that hard period of time unscathed.

The story was told to raise my awareness of the suffering around us. To my parents' dismay I was a rare fussy eater in a widespread famine era. With food being so scarce, my poor mother had to cater especially for me from my few acceptable vegetables she could count with one hand only. While the large saucepan was simmering for the entire family, one can always notice the tiny one next to it with fried potatoes. Unsurprisingly I maintained my chubby little frame which I was predisposed to from birth among the sea of skinny masses. There was no question that I ate all the cakes to satisfy my unquenchable sugar cravings.

Every month Father went to get our rations from the special food store, I followed him despite his resolute reluctance. We would queue behind many hollow-eyed people with sunken hungry cheeks. All eyes would be fixed on me the moment Father and I walked in. Some couldn't resist to ask Father what he fed me daily. That was undoubtedly Father's most embarrassing moments in life. He did his best to avoid going to the food store with me, but I still followed him all the same.

A few years later in school my classmates reflected on the time they ate tree leaves to suppress their hunger. Always the story teller, for once I was speechless. Since no matter how hard I tried, I was unable to recall a trace of such an ingredient from my diet. The few times I climbed up the cypress trees in our garden was to play hide and seek with my fun-loving brother. My best friend was satisfied that I was never starved. According to her there is no pain like hunger pain. Mother was amazed with the maturity and wisdom of other people's children, while Father advised me not to feel sorry for myself if dessert was missing occasionally from my dinner.

As I followed Father so often, naturally I became his interpreter despite some of the complex issues and terminology being far beyond my junior years. Once I burst into tears instantly after hearing that the official policy is to make us finally eat the same food like the Han Chinese. Realising the request for more flour in our rations was denied, Father held my hand and quietly walked out from the office. Though frustrated, Father patiently waited for me to regain my composure then assured me that we would carry on eating bread made with flour purchased from the black market. He also told me he did try to study Mandarin when he was young, but my worried grandmother understandably forbade him to travel to the other side of the mountain on daily basis. Locally there was no school that could teach him the official language. He felt deaf and dumb in a land where he could not explain himself personally, he even recalled our early years in Harbin during which some fraudsters made us pay a hefty electricity price with a fake bill.

I was told that Father was reciting Ayet from the Koran when he left this world. I phoned from London on 4th December and was assured that he would have his blood transfusion the next day, but in the morning when I reached out to my phone again he was already buried. The sheer distance, the different time zone and the swift burial all left me to believe that Father was buried alive. I was worried Father felt lonely without Mother to accompany him while scared in a dark and confined space. I wished he had a lamp and his duttar next to him to play a tune to cheer himself up and disperse the silence surrounding him. My husband didn't laugh at my crazy thoughts. He didn't even remind me how I used to find the ancient Egyptians burying their dead with so many of their belongings absurd. Suddenly I wanted the same for my father once he died, didn't I? Death is hard to deal with, so Egyptian's rituals strangely started making sense.

CHAPTER 2 MOTHER

If you are in a better place, with blue sky and beautiful lake; you would be the brightest star after a thunder, instead of laid to rest six feet under.

By the time Mother died she already suffered a decade-long dementia. During the last four years of her life, she was fed through a tube. Years after her death we are still debating if it was ethical or moral to interfere with the hand of fate. When it became obvious that her body started rejecting even the liquidized food, we made the conscious decision to stop feeding her. In the next few days Mother burst into laughter from time to time, as if relieved that the torturous force-feeding was finally over. As always, even without speech, Mother could handle the adversity more gracefully. The morning before her burial when I said my final goodbye to her, I was heartbroken to see my once beautiful mother resembled a skeleton. It was 2014, she was 91 years old, too.

Mother was also Atush born but Kashgar grown as my grandfather had a flourishing business there.

It was a very turbulent time in Uyghur history, many innocent business men were murdered with excuses by the nationalist Chinese government and the wealth was confiscated to pay the state expense. My grandfather was also arrested for execution, but was miraculously released later. I was told that his Russian ambassador friend helped him to escape the capital punishment. I can believe this narrative, since Stalin was the mastermind of Uyghur massacre. When Sheng Shicai, the pretend communist of Chinese Nationalist Governor in Xinjiang, complained about his massive budget deficit, the villainous Stalin advised him to get it from wealthy Uyghurs by planting crimes on them. That started the horror in the 1930s, since Sheng violently tortured and executed as many as 100,000, mainly wealthy Uyghurs to death.

Mother was brought up with the right to liberty, scarfless and often went to cinema to watch films imported from Russian Uzbekistan during her teenage years. She was forever accompanied by one of her brothers. On one occasion, my grandmother had to join her when the brothers couldn't make it. My moody grandmother was at pain to sit through a movie she didn't enjoy, subsequently was also loath never to endure the indecency of cinemagoers again. According to her there were so many men around her when she was leaving the cinema, a man touched her bosom while the other one groped her bottom to her disgust. I tend to think those may not be deliberate acts, just the crowd rushing to get out of the often very narrow cinema door without social distancing.

Radio was a luxury at those days and the ones who could afford bought it from Russian Central Asia. The music played on radio were usually recorded in Uzbekistan (I never know the difference between Uyghur and Uzbek, I also confuse Kazakh with Kyrgyz). Whenever my grandfather's favourite songs were played while he was away, my grandmother would order her children to turn the radio off in a hurry. With the radio turned off, she thought it was possible to freeze the music eternally till my grandfather was around to enjoy it.

In the 1940s, divorce by women's request was still discouraged in the patriarchal China. Considering a married daughter as spilled water, the Han Chinese would not even let abused daughters take refuge in their original homes for a short period. In contrast Uyghurs took good care of their vulnerable daughters, or may be too good on another thought. At those days it wasn't uncommon to see the divorced teenage girls dwell in their parents' residency, some even had a baby by the age of fifteen. Uyghur parents brought back their unhappy daughters home and dealt with the divorce themselves. The abused wife never had to face the violent husband again. It might have protected numerous victims, but certainly ended some good marriages just based on trivial bickering.

However that was not Mother's life, at the age of 24 she must be the oldest virgin in Kashgar. Mother was a hopeless romantic who didn't just reject many marriages recommended by her loving parents, she was also brave enough to propose to Father. After she wrote to my unsuspecting and humbled father, she was able to marry the love of her life. The affection they showered on each other made many Han Chinese in Harbin suspect they eloped to enjoy their forbidden love in this distant land. It didn't help as Father constantly referred to Mother as his *lover*. It wasn't Father's innovative way to declare how he was smitten with Mother, it was the Chinese authorities' attempt to replace the demeaning term men referred to their wives as, *Laopo* (old woman) with *Airen* (lover). Young couples took to the new trend like a duck to water, but among the hesitant middle-aged Father could be a pioneer. We were suitably embarrassed, but there was no stopping Father to carry on using the few rare Chinese words he could pronounce properly.

With fondness now, I remember my parents' happy marriage. It is like reading Turgenev's

Sketches from a Hunter's Album, to discover that his headstrong mother proposed to his mild-mannered father in feudal Russia. When the intrinsic charms triumph over the harsh environment, one knows no matter where you live, when you are born and what gender you are assigned to, human spirits are all the same! Some of us are just too indomitable and resourceful, we soar to the challenge and beyond to be the fearless master of our fate. The irony is that no matter how hard men try to put an eighteen year old girl down by labelling her *Laopo* upon marriage, which literally means an old woman in Chinese, they are still reluctantly compelled to accept single women as *girls* forever. That title still holds even if the women reached the ripe old age of eighty. There is no better way to flatter a single woman by calling her a girl rather than a spinster. One would never expect womanhood is glorified for those who choose not to tie the knot in the East.

Father had two unhappy marriages before he married Mother at the age of 34. After he lost my grandmother, his aunt more or less forced him to marry her own daughter, his first cousin. After they had a daughter together, the first wife had an affair with a fellow villager while Father was away for business. This gave Father a good reason to divorce her. His second wife was from a peculiar Uyghur tradition. As a businessman he had to spend long periods away from home, so he was able to marry a local woman temporarily and divorce her before he left that town. Usually this type of marriage should exist in wherever it happened and ended there (in Father's case it was Khotan), but the woman came to Atush a few months after Father left and handed his baby daughter to him. According to my second step sister's mother, she gave birth to twin girls, one died and Father had the surviving one. My stepsisters were brought up by my childless aunt while financially supported by Father.

After the arrival of the Chinese Communist party my grandfather had to seek refuge in Harbin. It is one of the far Eastern cities in China, with Manchurian origin. I always think my grandfather got the idea of going to Harbin from his Russian business associates or the ambassador, otherwise how could he know this Russian world within China that needed a week to travel there! It was like going to another planet for those days. Thus Mother suddenly lost her entire family, and it would take a month to receive a letter from such a remote place.

As a consequence my grandfather was an internally displaced refugee, fled to Harbin to escape prosecution three thousand miles away. After missing her parents for years, Mother plucked up enough courage to travel to Harbin with four young kids under the age of seven.

Unknowingly she thrusted us into a refugee world. Our journey started with a flight then a slower than car train, with a capacity of less than 30 miles per hour. In Beijing we had to transfer to an equally slow northern line train to reach Harbin.

For a few months Mother was on cloud nine after reuniting with her beloved parents, but did dread the precarious journey back home since it wasn't for the faint-hearted. How could she manage traversing the unnerving week long journey with four young children all over again, fairly unscathed? Her look of despair gave my grandparents the pleasure to persuade her for a realistic long term settlement in Harbin: "What to fear when your parents are by your side?", they said. Mother was convinced especially after Father also agreed to join us soon. Little did she contemplate that my grandfather would be arrested before long and taken forcibly back to Xinjiang, leaving my desolate parents to suffer more and suffer worse. Indirectly I was a refugee, and spent my early 25 years in a city nobody called home.

Harbin is nothing like any city anyone has ever known, since the whole existence of it is based on migrants. Most of the people in Harbin were from Shandong, an overcrowded province in eastern China. Two thirds the area of the UK territory, Shandong now boasts a population of a hundred million. With hardly enough resources for survival, people were mostly starving there in the past. One neighbour told me how they were reduced to planting vegetables on soil of any size, including the skimpy plot beside their window. In the Neolithic fashion, everything planted was useful to quench the hunger in Shandong. Like the Americans who flooded California in the 1930s, Shandongnese then rushed to Manchuria, the then rumoured Cockaigne of China. There was never a plenitude of job promises, it was all about its vast, rich land and the small Manchurian population.

One thing in common about refugees is the homesickness they felt. I heard it all: even if they have left hell behind, they always talked about it like a paradise lost. First there were my parents telling us about our beautiful and stunning homeland, they called it a rare gem hidden in the middle of Gobi and Taklimakan deserts. They said we Central Asians aren't hopelessly populous to dwell in the desert sand hut; the lush oasis is fertile enough to turn our life to the envy of our neighbors. They took pride in the hospitality of Uyghur people and the tasty fruit and vegetables the Siberia-like Harbin could never cultivate. Then there were my classmates, they boasted about the size of the peaches in Shandong. Actually they called it *Shandong the home,* in Chinese *Shandong Jia.* If *home is where the heart is,* then Harbin with its tranquility of haven was sadly a heartless city.

Harbin is one of the coldest cities in the world. When I was studying for my first degree in Harbin Civil Engineering University, the design temperature given to us was minus 29 degrees Celsius. Nevertheless, it is a beautiful city across the famous Songhua river. Summer time we would all end up there for swimming and with the Sun Island together the entire population of Harbin could make a day of it under the sunshine with ease during the holiday season.

In the extreme cold of Harbin's winter the Songhua becomes an ice-bound river, then two events will take place in this river. First one was Russians would break the ice in January and have the icy dipping. Even the thought of getting near to this icy river scared me, let alone go and watch it like many people did. Second one was the spring ice breaking, which usually happens in April. It would attract thousands of people to watch the ice being bombarded. Big ice chunks will start floating and then gradually melt, to make it possible for July swimming.

Just before I left Harbin in the early 1980s, the idea of Ice Lantern was born. I did visit it once or twice, but these days anyone can watch it on TV as an international event and the elaborate design is just amazing. All these seems not enough to impress the Shandongese, I spent my school days hearing my classmates praising the incredible *Shandong*

Jia. My friends told me the sea there is shimmering green, not blue, definitely nothing like the muddy Songhua river. For refugees, there is just no place like home, and nothing can ease the pain of being uprooted.

Harbin is a young city, it was a fishing village at the turn of last century, then came the Russians to escape from the October Revolution. These Russians called themselves White Russians. Though Belarus means white Russia in Russian language, these Russian refugees were not from there. The white here means not red, not revolutionary and with an aristocratic claim. It is like denying Bolsheviks their Caucasian identity. These wealthy Russians arrived with wagons full of gold coins with Tsar Nicholas's head engraved on them. This is the money built Harbin and in a style for Harbin to be called Eastern Paris.

Russian culture was dominant in Harbin. I was brought up in a Russian kindergarten; what I really hated there was the cabbage soup, otherwise it was fun. Singing and dancing was our daily activities, so we could perform to our parents during Christmas and Easter. I am really proud when no one would dance with a limping Russian boy, I volunteered to be his partner. However he didn't turn up on performance day for obvious reasons, and I had to improvise to make the dance resemble a solo performance. There was a point we had to link our hands, I made an effort to make it looked natural. I wasn't given any credit for my innovation; at the age of only five I could already feel that our dance was never being taken seriously because of my partner's disability status.

There was a cinema with films imported from the Soviet Union only for the Russians to watch, and a bakery where we could buy Russian rye bread. As the only Uyghur family we tried to get involved, not remain as outsiders. We had chosen Russians to belong to, since we eat bread and butter like them. We were accepted as one of them together with the Tatars, Jewish, Polish and even a Serbian among this group; we called him Yugoslavian then. We spoke Russian and everyone sent their children to study with an old Russian teacher, Maria Ivanovo. There were not many kids though, since the ones who got children mostly immigrated to America or Australia for the sake of better education.

My parents sent us to the local state primary school, because they wanted us to get an all-round education, not just develop simple arithmetic and language skills. My parents remained in Harbin even after all the other Uyghur families went back to Xinjiang voluntarily or forcibly. My grandfather was arrested and taken back with handcuffs after the government got a tip-off from his evil daughter-in-law. The police kept the handcuffs during the entire journey, it lasted more than a week and he was thrown into jail as soon as they reached Urumqi. He was released from prison three days before his death in a dying state, all for the crime of being rich before the communists took over China.

Father was not arrested because he didn't own any land in his life time. My paternal grandfather died a few years before Communist took over China. As a result the house and land left behind was divided among five siblings, and Father gave his share to his brother since he didn't live in Atush anymore. My unfortunate uncle was classified as a landlord, then endured enormous suffering. His only son even lost his eyesight, since he was denied medical treatment. The other thing Father did right was he never got involved in any business after communists banned it. The true communist government of those days had none of the business savvy charm of today's Chinese rulers. Being rich was a crime, starting a business deserved punishment. I was made to feel guilty forever in school for having a rich grandfather.

For the first ten years in Harbin, we lived off Father's savings from the past. By the 1960s, when the money ran low, Father had to start working hard in his Russian styled dairy farm to provide for us. It wasn't an easy life, he had to get up every morning at 3 am to feed and milk the cows, but as someone who didn't speak Chinese, Father was naturally unemployable. It was a poverty stricken time in China, even famine; milk and butter at least kept us going. Slowly Father had fallen in love with his farm, he worked hard and was proud that he could offer families with babies and sick ones fresh milk, something the government was unable to supply. As a result, we became famous in Harbin with the high-quality milk we provided to people around us. Ours must be the only whole milk, neither skimmed nor tempered with water on sale in Harbin at that time.

Mother decided to put up with the hardship so we could be better educated. Unable to speak Chinese and with limited Russian, life was not easy, not to mention how homesick my parents were. However, the start of the Cultural Revolution shattered our educational dream. Schools initially became a fun ground for rebellious pupils to denounce their teachers, then when education resumed we just recited Chairman Mao's words. To make sure that we didn't waste our formative years playing in the streets and learning nothing in school, my parents sent the four of us to study with Marivanna (that was what we called Maria Ivanovo). I learned my English from her and later was able to obtain a grant from the British Council to study for a master's degree in Imperial College, thanks to her successful teaching.

Marivanna was a widow and not wealthy like other White Russians. She relied on her teaching income for survival. She was full of praise for her Tsar's army general husband. The fact that he was not loaded with the gold coins shared by Russians when they arrived at Harbin did indicate his dedication to his career instead of wealth. He was murdered in 1945, when the Russian Red Army liberated Manchuria from Japanese occupation as soon as Germany surrendered. Stalin sent his soldiers around Harbin to arrest any White Russians who served the Tsar in the past, in a similar fashion like many autocratic governments punishing the collaborators from the previous regime. One winter night the general went to answer the door and was hit by a hammer on his head. He died several days later in the hospital.

One of my parents' Russian friends called Shander was having tea with his brother one afternoon during 1945. The door was pushed open and a few Russian Red Army officers came in to ask for Shander. Although both of them bear the same surname, it was our family friend they were after. As a quick thinker (at least faster than his kinder brother), our friend got up from his seat and pointed to his brother as the Shander then made his swift exit from his own home. He survived and his brother was executed instead of him. Mother was in awe of their unusually smart friend while

I considered him as an evil man after the story of his survival surfaced and even stopped greeting him. The last time I saw him was at Marivanna's funeral in 1973. Shander was probably 90 then, albeit a very fit one.

With *the children to tend, the clothes to mend, the floor to mop, the food to shop,* my early memory of Mother started with her always on the go. Being a perfect homemaker was her care and delight. However she was more than that too, as she continued searching for extraordinary ways to enrich our lives. It was a time all mothers owned sewing machines and made clothes for their offspring, but what Mother made were not simply fit to wear but also fetchingly prettier. To achieve that, she went through the trouble to learn how to make embroidered dresses and blouses from a Russian woman we subsequently nicknamed Madam Flora. Mother graduated into an embroidery artist. She sent us, her three daughters, to school with glamorous dresses had embroidery sewn down the front and side, she even covered our windows with embroidered curtains containing many little holes. After she produced tablecloths with sweet dainty decorations she still got the energy left to learn knitting jumpers for us from a Japanese woman.

To Father's great pleasure Mother cooked Uzbek pilau for us every week. Father would fondly remind us that the Soviet leader Nikita Khrushchev invited President Kennedy to visit Russia during his trip to America, with the promise of serving him the Uzbek pilau. Apparently Khrushchev was a fan of Uzbek pilau, just like Father. Mother also made the *laghman* which Boris Johnson called slimy noodles from his Uzbekistan holiday. Our Han Chinese friends were all immensely impressed with Mother's Uyghur noodles, some even suggested that Marco Polo must have learnt the trade from us then took the pasta back to the Italians for further development.

It was quite edifying to see Mother not satisfied by keeping an orderly home but trying to extend her cooking range to include the Chinese stir-fries. One of our family friends, a Dungan woman (Chinese Muslim, descendants of Arabic father and Han Chinese mother) was invited to teach Mother the skill, yet it didn't inspire Mother to explore the Chinese cooking further. According to Mother her mentor relied on deep frying and oceans of oil to achieve the desirable flavour. Up to that day I always considered Chinese cuisine as healthier than Uyghur's; now Mother presented another scenario. Probably it was the Han Chinese banquet Mother was taught to prepare - we are after the healthy daily dishes.

What Mother excelled in was when she learned to bake Russian cakes. The amazing Madam Flora was also an accomplished Madam for Russian desserts to our contentment. As always Madam Flora didn't disappoint, while the ever-evolving Mother had almost managed to transform herself from an industrious housewife to a culinary artist specialized in pastry. Soon Mother filled our dinner table with mouth-watering delicious Russian cakes. Even today I can impress friends and neighbors with my Russian caramel layered crispy walnut cake. As someone with a sweet tooth, I was delighted to see the sweet treat during festive and birthday seasons. I felt grateful for Mother's effort, she might have set aside her own dreams to share ours only. We thrived but she had to cope with dementia in her eighties, which made her unable to continue learning new skills and life stopped being fun for her anymore.

Mother often traveled back to Urumqi, the capital city of Xinjiang to visit her own mother, brothers and sisters. After missing her for a few months, we would welcome Mother back with wonderful nuts and dried fruits that can only be found in Central Asia. She brought back a lot of information too. One of Mother's stories was chilling, some Uyghurs were executed as members of the Eastern Turkestan movement. Among them there was a middle-aged man called Tohti Kurban. In a public rally before the execution, when his name was called as the one to be executed by fire squats, he lifted his head and stared at the crowd with a dignified look for the last time. I assume his hands were tied at the back and an angry policeman must be pushing his head down which was a familiar scene very often witnessed by us school children at such rallies. I cried for the courageous freedom fighter, or maybe just a man who innocently talked about our independence during social events. Such executions were always staged as a deterrent to the others without any trial.

Being colonized is a bitter pill to swallow: you live in an appallingly imbalanced society, and are forced to watch the annihilation of your beloved culture from the socially inferior footing assigned to you. As a consequence we Uyghurs had been dreaming for our independence, which is a holy grail we have been paying a very heavy price for. Father's Uyghur nationalist teacher, Memtili Efendi was murdered by the Chinese authority in the 1930s for daring to instill national self-consciousness in his students. Worse yet, a 23-year-old Uyghur poet Li'Mutellip was butchered with the guillotine for simply writing about our independent future. He was chopped from his feet onward until he passed out in pain and finally died. The heroic splendour of the young poet strengthened our desire for freedom even when barbaric punishment loomed large in the vicinity. The silence Chinese authorities imposed on us only deprived us from public discourse about independence.

Desperate for freedom we tried our luck with independence, always with the same outcome at perilous cost. In the Battle of Kashgar, Chinese revenge killing turned the river red with blood from five thousand Uyghurs'. The majority of them were horrified women and children, who weren't even allowed to sit their lives out innocently. It was named *Kizil Massacre* in the history, *kizil* is the Turkic word for red. We flexed our muscles again in the 1940s under servile living conditions. In mainland China, the civil war was raging and the outwardly more sentient and less corrupt Communists set to win. We thought getting rid of the Nationalist Chinese would get us a step closer to independence which Chairman Mao promised us in Yanan, not known to us then that keeping promises is never high on Communist's agenda. Besides the civil warring parties may have failed to compromise on all other issues, but they were firmly united on the colonial front: the unspoken agreement was that *the winner takes it all.*

It didn't help that even Russians turned to the Chinese side. It instilled a sense of hopelessness in me, as if we Central Asians are forsaken by God, or at least not on the radar of God's interest. Otherwise how can one explain Stalin's allergy to an independent Uyghur state! With an extra helping hand from Russians, the Japanese were pushed out of China and we were kept within the Chinese territory. Under the communist regime we have even lost the right to make a mind trip towards our independence, let alone to file a complaint of unfulfilled promise and duplicity. Peculiarly, the Chinese occupation of our immense agricultural and mineral wealth has gone unnoticed and uncontested by outside world until now. Even Edward Said, the prominent late academic of postcolonial studies declared more than two decades ago that the direct colonialism has largely ended. In the history of war ours might sound incidental and short but no less perilous to us as it was painful to some of the Han Chinese settlers there.

One afternoon in 1947, my uncle's door was pushed open and a screaming little girl rushed in then pulled my uncle's hands with all her might. Though he couldn't understand her Chinese, my uncle did recognize that she was the four-year-old daughter of his Han Chinese neighbour. Following her to her home, my uncle found a young Uyghur man pointing his gun on the girl's father in their kitchen. With the girl in hysteria, my uncle asked the young man to put his weapon down. He also explained to the youngster (only in his late teens) that this was a good Han Chinese. Maybe that was all the nervous assassin needed, he was unable to pull the trigger all along. He left with his gun, hopefully didn't murder anyone later. My uncle's panic-stricken neighbour started packing without a moment's delay and left Xinjiang with his daughter on that same day.

I like the second part of the story more. It was 1957, my businessman uncle strolled around Huangpu district, the city center of Shanghai. Suddenly a man grabbed him from behind and shouted: "After ten years, I have found you at last". By then my uncle learnt to speak a bit of Chinese. It was the neighbour from ten years ago hugging him now. He had been examining every Uyghur man's face in Shanghai for an entire decade in his search for the saviour. An incredible act. He took my uncle home and introduced him to all his family, apparently apart from his wife and daughter he also had many siblings. For the next two weeks, my uncle had been invited to banquets by the neighbour's brothers and sisters in turn. The hospitality and gratitude they had shown were quite over the top. My uncle realized theirs was a well-off family and wondered what a man from such a prosperous background was doing in Xinjiang. It has always been seen as a promised land by the economical Han Chinese refugees. Some might have skills to offer, but the majority only have survival dreams to fulfil.

I worshiped my uncle from the moment I heard his story and was eager to meet him. In 1969 my dream had finally come true when mother took me to Urumqi. The first thing I asked was about his conspicuous bravery. My passionate narration of what I received from Mother certainly called forth Uncle's fond memories. A soft-spoken man, Uncle wasted no words to cover himself with glory of courage. Instead, he talked about his delight to meet up with the neighbour later, and expressed his pleasure to know that the man was doing well in Shanghai. However the same couldn't be said about him. Soon Uncle was arrested for doing business in Shanghai and was sent to prison together with my grandfather. He trained as a dentist upon his release four years later and was favoured by many with his renowned practice. His contribution to the local community's oral health was invaluable at a time in tumultuous China, when people struggled to get any medical treatments for the lack of hospitals and doctors. He left this world in 2009, five years before my mother, his favourite sister's death. Uncle was 92 and a hero of mine forever.

Not all the war casualties were so lucky, and not all the bloodshed guarantees independence unfailingly. When Russian Central Asia gained their independence in the early 1990s, Dalai Lama predicted Tibet, Mongols and Uyghurs would rule their own country next, but it is not meant to be. If Russia let their Central Asians Republics go for the fear of declining Russian population, and the consequence of becoming minority inside the Soviet Union, the Han Chinese has no such worry. The Han Chinese makes up 94% of the Chinese population, and would remain so for the foreseeable future. The surplus Chinese population always find their way to our town and cities in a hurry, while taunting us for the lack of multi-story buildings before their arrival. Only if they knew how we miss our bungalow-only days, with an open view and clean air.

To *adore God with joy* wasn't in the realm of Mother's living experience. Despite Father's profound influence and Mother's strong desire never to disobey him, she was only a half-hearted Muslim from my observation. She went to Hajj with Father just to look after him and to see the world of course. When Father was reading his Koran, Mother would read her endless romance fictions sitting next to him. It was Mother's loyal friend's duty to send her a dozen of novels each year from Urumqi. These were books published in Uzbekistan and ended up in Xinjiang bookshops. What Father and Mother relished together was reading the Xinjiang Daily newspaper. It was a week-old news when it reached Harbin and unquestionably the government's mouthpiece, yet my parents were able to discuss and infer a lot of information out of the articles. It gave them tremendous pleasure to be acquainted with world affairs just by scouring whatever writings were at hand.

It was a time of menacing Russian and Chinese conflict, as *revisionist* Russians were more condemned than the *imperialist* Americans. After Chairman Mao urgently asked the country to store more food, everyone feared the start of an imminent war. Our school days were passed digging tunnels, people were even asked to stick stripy tapes on the window to avoid injury from bomb-shattered glass. Yet my parents could find no traces of such danger from their newspapers. They could see the hostility was only lip service and concluded that two gigantic communist countries would never rip each other into pieces with war to entertain America. And not to forget that the war in Vietnam was fought with Russian weapons and Chinese manpower, so the cooperation continued.

Through reading newspapers my parents became fans of Fidel Castro. As all the publications in China, only the authorities' favourites can gain inches in papers, so we never heard of Che Guevara. Seeing Castro settled for Cuban leadership and left the jungle guerrilla warfare to the ultraistic and heroic Che alone, the Chinese leaders felt safe in Castro's company. My parents didn't just enjoy to watch cute Cuba challenged the almighty America, they also adored Castro for not shying away from criticizing the two largest communist countries who had been supporting him financially all along. Father would devoutly quote that Castro angrily called the war in Vietnam a gift to the imperialists and disaster to the Vietnamese people, as he hated to see the self-serving world powers settling their scores there. China either didn't get the hint of the accusation, or just conveniently ruled themselves out as too innocent to be a modern-day imperialist. The quotation was printed anyway to pin the blame squarely on America and Russia for the unfair warfare.

Growing up in an environment like that, it was just natural for me to end up being Fidel Castro's admirer too despite hating the Cuban sugar which we were forced to buy a packet of if granulated sugar was purchased. The unrefined brown sugar was not appreciated for its healthy nature in China during those days. Luckily soon this sugar had disappeared from the market, but so did charismatic Fidel Castro. Since the Soviet Union used the Cuban Crisis to pressure American recognition of Cuba, the grateful Fidel Castro subsequently ditched China for bickering with Russia. Now Chairman Mao was only left with little friends (like Albania), a girl friend (Sirimavo Bandaranaike, prime minister of Ceylon, present day Sir Lanka) and black friends from Africa. Mother told me the person who coined this phrase was jailed for his disrespectful act towards Chairman Mao, actually for humiliating China.

All good things come to an end, soon Father and Mother could no longer have fun with words from newspapers anymore. In 1969 the Chinese government proudly announced that they had helped Uyghurs to make the momentous leap by creating a modern script for us. The official line was that Uyghurs were backwards no more, a Latin script now would advance our culture. I loved the new script and wished Father spent some time to learn it so he could carry on enjoying his newspapers, but he thought it was too hard for him to adapt.

Fourteen years passed, and the new script was scrapped in 1983 back to the Arabic one. When I was teaching structural engineering in the Xinjiang Technological College, my students used to answer the exam questions in Chinese, Uyghur Latin script or even Arabic script. They also complained about how changing script can pull a nation twenty years backwards. Anyway, they are the victims, the students must be in a good position to appraise such a hopeless predicament. Hailed once as a stepping stone into the modern world, are we back to ancient civilization zone? No comments from the Chinese authorities this time. No wonder Arabs love the Chinese. Sometimes I feel we Uyghurs are Frankenstein's Monster in Arabic making. Halfway during our history, the Arabs came to impose their culture and religion to us, so we gave up our script and belief. But instead of nurturing us, when the Chinese prosecuted us for adopting Islamic culture, Arabs just cheered and are still cheering.

By the time we left Harbin after spending a quarter of a century there, the Shandongese were already rooted and might have abandoned their strange, hard-to-comprehend accent. We baby boomers were taught to speak the standard Mandarin in school, which is so pleasing to the ear, even a Beijing accent sounds coarse in comparison. Does anyone still visit *Shandong Jia?* Perhaps as a holiday destination only. As the only Uyghur family there, we never intended to make Harbin our permanent home. Years later I told Mother that my dreams were always about our life in Harbin, she just indifferently said 'Ah'. There was no asking what my dreams were about, probably it was too much pain for her to look back. Mother's memories about Harbin might be all about how my grandfather was dragged away with handcuffs.

My grandmother who was born at the end of the 19th century died in 1981. A month after Mother retuned from her funeral, we received a telegram claiming my uncle also died. Mother had two brothers and we had to go to the telecommunications center to find out which brother died by making a long-distance call. It was my older uncle, who was lonely and poverty-stricken. Unable to hold down a job and with no inheritance from my grandmother, he died in a seasonal epidemic which struck Kashgar every year. He was in his 60s, in poor health and just back from my grandmother's funeral when he took ill. All these sad events must have filled up Mother's memory with sorrowful flashbacks. Mother spent her later years sinking into her deep thoughts and constantly staring out of the windows. Even her favourite novels lost their attraction slowly. We are not sure when exactly the decline of her brain started, since we simply put it down to depression initially. When she was finally diagnosed, that demeaning Chinese phrase for dementia, *old age moron,* brought vast discomfort to us.

Mother developed asthma in the long and harsh Harbin winters, like many locals there. Her asthma tormented her more during cold winter nights, as a result I used to worry her frail body would give in during one of those asthma attacks. It started up Mother's addiction to painkillers, and what an addiction it was! Did the excessive amount of painkillers messed up her brain? We would never know. Her asthma attacks were the unpleasant, even chilling episodes in my otherwise very happy childhood. I accept that the drug must have helped Mother to tolerate her breathing problem, while the chest pain was precarious enough to push people to end their own lives during their struggle to breathe. But pondering the danger of developing dementia, I have decided not to take painkillers all my life. I would let the pain take its own course (luckily not that many so far) and drew my GP husband to despair very often by refusing his help.

It was Mother's life journey that took us to Harbin, I had witnessed the redirection power of economic or political situations as a refugee. These days refugees have become the equivalent of opportunists in our vocabulary and are unwanted by the locals of any country. The truth of refugees' stories is often about courage, resilience, about willingness to uproot from the deep generation nest and enter an imaginary comfort zone. The aftermath of the migrants' venture is an enriched local culture and prosperous provincial economy. It is this very reality which has shaped our world inordinately so that no country is an island on its own anymore.

CHAPTER 3 IBRAHIM

If time will ease my pain, I should have no tear when I hear your name; my heart is still in a million pieces, instead of strolling down memory lane.

Ibrahim is my only brother who was born on 1st May 1952, according to Mother exactly three years before I entered this world. Or was it? I was born after midnight, so it must count as 2nd of May, but in a country that didn't even issue birth certificates, it never mattered. I remember Father was unimpressed when I gushed about the wonder of so many Uyghurs to become centenarians while reading the newspaper. According to Father those deluded old people hadn't got a clue of their age, they just simply made the hundred year age up. The protagonist Rasheed in *A Thousand Splendid Suns* thought he was 75 years old near the end of his life, then Khaled Hossaini admitted the truth was that Rasheed didn't even know how old he was - I could draw the parallel to support Father's theory. Age is a myth in Central Asia, once people used to rely on the major earthquake at the end of the 19th century to indicate their lives started before or after that disaster. The age confusion was actually beyond us, no one ever saw a birth certificate from China and its neighbours at large until recently.

Ibrahim was five years old when we arrived in Harbin and he was able to start playing with the Han Chinese children in the street straight away. Language was no barrier to children, he learnt to swear in Chinese so fast before Mother could even contemplate what he was uttering. It must be an infantile defense mechanism to enable children to start swiftly communicating and dealing with the bullies on the identical level, with the same language. Father was in Shanghai at that time, otherwise the scholarly-mannered him could have been horrified. Ibrahim was Father's very sought-after son, arrived after Father had three daughters from three different marriages already. Ibrahim was also my grandfather's name. In Uyghur tradition Father named his first and ultimately only son after his own father.

Father was in jail when his precious son was born, charged for the fraud he never committed. He was thrown into a prison cell with a Han Chinese inmate. They were unable to communicate but Father could sense his cellmate was innocent too. Father often saw him being taken out for interrogation and thrown back to the cell in a lifeless state. Through gestures Father understood he was tortured with a wooden log pressed forcefully on the back of his knees. It would take the poor man a long time to recover, then the same torture was repeated. To avoid the painful torment himself, Father accepted all the charges and spent his days praying in a corner.

After one year Father was taken out for interrogation. This time it was different - a thin and tall Han Chinese with an army officer's uniform was there to question him. From the way everyone kowtowed at him Father sensed he was a high-ranking official with a decisive voice. Years later Father found out he was Wang Zhen, the top Chinese leader in Xinjiang and one of the veterans of the Chinese Communist Party. Father told Wang Zhen through interpreter that he never committed such a crime. 'But you confessed' roared back Wang Zhen. He narrowed his eyes at the same time, as if intimidating Father with a vision of power could peer through his mind. Father calmly told him the confession was to protect himself, to not suffer like his cellmate. Suddenly Wang Zhen started screaming in such a rage. He waved his arms, hit the table and pointed to some of his lower rank officers furiously. Father could see the subordinates were not just unable to answer back to their boss, they even shivered under his fuming gaze. Their frightful downcast glare made it obvious that Wang Zhen was accustomed to treating his inferiors rudely and violently in all situations.

Father was released the next day. Communist China is no less feudal, a decision about life and death is never based on law or justice. Leaders declare themselves, and are always greeted by obedient acceptance. The same Wang Zhen could have had Father executed, like he did to many thousands of Uyghurs in the early 1950s, but Father was lucky to be let go, maybe because the allegation wasn't political. During our school days, we were often taken to the cinema for movies which were preceded by documentaries of Chinese leaders, who we were told were busy designing our bright future. Whenever I saw Wang Zhen among the other communist politburo members, the image of him angrily shouting to Father would play in my head. A philistine warmonger, he mutated into a scheme-hatching politician with an aura of invincibility.

Father was finally able to hug his son, not just briefly looking at Ibrahim during the prison visit when he was held by Mother. Father hoped for another son but had two more daughters instead. When I was born he only got a boy's name ready for me. My aunt, who had fair share of misfortune in her life, named me Melike. It is Arabic for princess, to reverse my bad luck. It did the trick - I became daddy's girl a few months after I was born.

Years later, Father told me that he never knew daughters could be so interesting and caring at the same time. He enjoyed our company so much and watched the women in his life dominate the family plot with satisfaction.

When Ibrahim was seven years old, it was time for his circumcision. A simple procedure for Uyghur boys turned into a calamity for my brother. Among the not-circumcising Han Chinese, Mother felt lucky when a Jewish doctor came to our rescue. The doctor did the cutting without any anesthesia as he couldn't own such facilities in China during that era, with Ibrahim kicking and screaming, then he left after the operated organ was bandaged. That night Ibrahim had a fever, then received a new bandage from the doctor after the wound was cleaned the following day. God knows how many times the indomitable doctor came back to deal with the aftermath, since a month later Ibrahim was still bedbound and crying. That led Mother to emulate the Uyghur approach to circumcision by taking the bandage off, which enabled the wound to dry and led to consequent healing. Finally Ibrahim was able to resume his old life. I assume it was the first time for this doctor to perform circumcision on a rebellious boy; the Jewish boys have the procedure completed during their early and easy infancy.

Ibrahim grew up fast. Parents' meeting at school

posed a problem for me – the teacher always complained for the no show of my non-Mandarin-speaking parents. When Ibrahim was eleven I brought him in, but he was too shy to face the challenge, hence he remained at the school gate. When the teacher came out to get him, she found Ibrahim was coyly hiding behind a tree. He was dismissed. Two years later, a new teacher and relentless new demand forced me to bring Ibrahim in again. Now puberty had kicked in, Ibrahim was a few inches taller, looked mature and confident with his newly developing moustache. He walked into the classroom with me promptly and the teacher even sprang up on her feet to shake the 13-year old's hand. He must have looked 30, since facial hair is so uncommon among the Han Chinese.

The teacher finally found someone to pour her heart out to about my unruly behaviour. She expressed her serious doubts that I would ever be a great proletariat. She was upset I kept reading books not suitable for little girls, like the *Song of Youth,* and even corrupted my classmates by turning the book into endless enticing little tales. Now many parents were complaining about my bad influence, since their children wanted to read the forbidden book too. Moreover, the teacher was horrified I could even get my hands on Western books, such as *Pride and Prejudice.* 'How could your parents allow Melike to continue her decline on this slippery bourgeoisie slope?' she concluded at last.

What the teacher didn't know was that I could have preferred to read *The Secret Diary of Adrian Mole Aged 13¾*, but Sue Townsend had yet to pen it two decades later. The books I read (or managed to lay my hands on) may be too romantic for the teacher's liking but she overlooked their revolutionary content. Lin Daojing and Elizabeth Bennett both rejected arranged marriage, finally Lin courageously joined the anti-Japanese occupation movement in Beijing whereas Elizabeth was able to attract the arrogant Mr. Darcy to her orbit with her eloquence and witty manner. These were women ahead of their time, but couldn't be considered as little girls' role models during the Cultural Revolution. The teacher was an ardent follower of Chairman Mao. She arrogantly presented us Mao's poem, claiming Genghis Khan was only fit to hunt the birds, so Elizabeth Bennett must be nothing more than a social climber to her.

My credulous brother, who was never an eager student himself, promised the teacher that now my parents knew what I was up to, they would never allow me to carry on reading those books in the future, as if I was learning how to rob a bank. Much to Ibrahim's disappointment, my parents just shrugged off the bad school report, rather they were more concerned about Ibrahim skipping school. One autumn, his teacher complained that he didn't attend school for an entire summer. My unsuspecting parents only then realised that he went swimming every day with his equally naughty classmates. Every morning they headed straight to the Songhua River with school bags still on their shoulders. With its fierce current, two young lives were lost on a daily basis in the summertime at Songhua River, as if there was a selfish sea monster beneath demanding teenagers to be sacrificed for his pleasure. A nightmare river for all parents in Harbin, not to mention the educational opportunities Ibrahim had missed.

Luckily Ibrahim got stronger and better as his swimming went on behind my parents' back. Or so it seemed, otherwise how could he had frequently crossed to the other side of this unfriendly river and back safely? He wanted me to experience the thrill too, but I was hopeless to start with and once was almost swept away by the strong current. Besides I would rather put some effort to get on the good side of the teacher's and stop her staring at me with dislikes. However, it didn't take long for me to realise that the teacher had been spot on with her prediction. I was resolutely rejected by the Communist Youth League in secondary school. No communist party members ever approached me at university either, that is how potential party member candidates are groomed. As if everyone knew that I wished Karl Marx was never born and blamed Marxism for all the sadness in the world. Though it became clear to me later that it was just a matter of time for someone else to express the same idea, I refused to warm up to the kingpin of communism.

Utopia is forever consciously sought after by daydreamers, a fine dinner party topic maybe, but a sheer horror for those who live under the experiment. The theory in practice must have lost some of its ancestral spark due to the different adaptation from many communist states. Based on their own special circumstances China felt accomplished after distributing the wealth from the landowners to all villagers, while the Soviet Union grappled with their all-powerful rich farmers. Whereas Chinese peasants were confined in the People's Communes, Soviet farmers were grouped in Collective Farms. But one thing they got in common is that none of the countries that practiced communism has so far managed to create a world that outsiders like to enter.

People assume everyone in a communist country believes in communism. In reality, only the members of the communist party adopt that thought, or at least pretend that the dogma is coherently divine with a solid foundation. The party members make up about five percent of the general population, but are the pillars of the

Communist society of China while the remaining 95% are relegated to the fate of the castoffs. Such is the rigid social order laid out for the *aristocrats* and *plebs* of communism. Beneath the lust for the acquisition of communist membership is not the yearning for the recognition of one's achievement, but always the desire for extra wealth and power. It might sound absurd that the camp-followers are expected to look upon the party leadership as a prophet, but with endless privilege as reward, it is hard for many to resist.

It was Stalin who declared that communist party members were made of special stuff. As someone who aptly named himself as semantically Russian steel, Stalin once famously refused to exchange the German general in his captive with his Nazi prisoner son during The Second World War. Even the execution of his son couldn't stop the little troubled Soviet leader from going about his governance business as usual through sheer steely willpower. I was brought up watching mini-Stalins filled out the Chinese silver screens. These wartime heroes either quietly endured surgical procedure without general anesthetic, or fearlessly cried out 'long live Chairman Mao' before their own execution. Without the melodrama of wartime, the party members evolved into very socially skilled individuals, who appear to be popular and hidden behind a harmonious exterior with their environment.

They aren't supposed to complain and must smile even when they are fazed. They worked hard and never challenged their bosses before they attained their party memberships. It is an open secret to bribe the local party boss to be a qualifier, but it has to be done tastefully, discreetly, never clumsily.

Desperate to join the communist party, a friend of mine took the trouble to please her boss in the bedroom, yet it backfired. She lost her dignity and was never offered a party membership. The sleazy (and ugly) boss must have tricked her when she was at her most vulnerable while focusing on her goal precariously. In a time when female reputation was based on her chastity only, she was viewed as someone with a tainted past. She needed a lot of courage and resilience to survive the aftermath of her spectacular failure, as all people including the man she married later called her *damaged goods*. Tragedy like this was common in China at those days. Combining the disparate feudalistic characteristics of Chinese society with communism, men's power was extended while the female branch of the society was eternally stuck in the lawless dark alleys. The toxic regime terminated countless angelic dreams and subsequently cost many innocent young lives too.

For most people in China, communism remains a hazy concept with many impossible contradictions. The gripping narrative offered to us is that human history starts from the slave society, progresses to feudal, the capitalist, socialist and finally bingo: communist world. China was in the socialist stage, that means the wealthy Western capitalist regimes were trailing behind us. Then the bubble burst in 1980 when China *downgraded* itself into the capitalist system and consequently progressed into a wealthy state. Not feeling the defeat or letdown, the government carries on telling people that the future of our planet is red, as the supreme communist way of life will be enjoyed eventually by the entire human race. No need to work for a living in a fancy communist Eden, but the spectacle is in the sense that you will work anyway as it shall become your first need. For someone whose first need of the day is forever a morning cup of coffee, I am relieved that I will not be around then.

I was brought up in an innocent era when the communist authorities knew not of our skepticism and their ideology yet to be tarnished. Though it didn't take long to outwit the rudimentary concept of the hopeless truth that government preferred. My disdain for the cruelty of Communism was also amplified by seeing the suffering the doctrines brought upon my parents. It is impossible not to relate to the tragic pain my parents endured with so much heaviness in my heart. Mother wept with agony whenever she talked about her father's harrowing death; Father felt profound contempt for those who murdered his mentor simply for the crime of educating Uyghur youths in the 1930s under the communist banner. But it wasn't hate my parents taught me, instead they asked me to challenge every single word the teachers said reticently. They even showed me how to unearth the truth between the lines from propaganda filled newspapers.

Ibrahim wasn't remotely interested in communist membership, he hated the repressive dogma of communism. He joked about the stern-looking communist members and preferred to sweet talk his way out of any circumstances. His sense of humour was at stark contrast to the tough-talking bosses and their claim that communism was here with a mission to rescue humankind. I think a lot of political dictums were lost in translation when it reached Ibrahim. An essay he wrote during his primary school days made me chuckle for years. The Chinese soldiers who fought the Korean war were hailed as *the most beloved* people to celebrate the triumphant feelings of the authorities, yet Ibrahim named Mother as his most adored person in his essay. He might be voicing the universal truth, but the teacher expected an article about war heroes, not commoners like parents. It wasn't in Ibrahim's nature to challenge the educational establishment with facts, he must be daydreaming while the teacher outlined the criteria and penned a true to title essay to thank our loving and caring mother when the deadline approached.

Besides, Ibrahim hated anything involving hard work. He was more a playboy, always surrounded by female admirers because of his good looks. He reminds me of Bao Yu from the *Dream of The Red Chamber*[2]. Like Bao Yu he was a feminist, and must have felt purified and invigorated with girls as he considered them as pure as water. However Ibrahim didn't view men as clay in Bao Yu's manner, unknowingly he once mingled with a wrong crowd for a short period, but left the gang as he realized they were a violent lot.

Ibrahim didn't just despise those devoid of compassion, there was also his kind tenderness towards animals, that laid deep in the core of his heart. When Marivanna's two German Shepherds were being murdered, he cried a lot. It was the beginning of the Cultural Revolution, a group of thugs stormed into Marivanna's house and took the dogs out to hang them on the elm tree just outside her window. Instead of dealing with rabies, the government then just simply banned people from having canines, but foreign citizens were exempted from it. Unfortunately at a lawless period when rule books were all torn up. We all loved those dogs, two gentle creatures who welcomed us every time when we entered the house. They were Marivanna's best friends, the poor woman now only got us, her students as her company. Ibrahim tried his best to console our traumatized sister with solacing words, who unfortunately saw the poor dogs' bodies dangling under the elm tree.

One of our Dungan friends was a prominent doctor. One rainy night about thirty Red Guards burst into their house and occupied it for the next two months. The doctor with his elderly parents, wife and four children were confined into a small garden shed while the Red Guards stayed in their luxurious house and trashed it. The doctor and his father were constantly beaten for not revealing the gold and even a dead body which the Red Guards claimed was buried in the garden. The youngsters spent their days digging up the entire garden, they even dug under the bedroom and kitchen floor in vain.

After two futile months, with nonstop bickering between the teenagers, fed up with communal life, and probably missed their parents and home cooking, the Red Guards decided to call it a day when even the violent ones couldn't extract any further fun from it. They left behind a ruined house, a paralyzed old man due to their continuous torture and a houseful of broken hearts. Later I wanted to know how these young criminals managed to get into their house, I was told one of them knocked at the door asking for temporary shelter from the rain. They all rushed in as soon as the door opened, but the doctor admitted that even if they refused to open the door the violent crowd would break in with the axes they brought along with them.

Events like these were not exactly the authorities' doing, but the police didn't have the power to stop them unfolding either. It must have started with the youngsters' rush of blood to their brain when they were trying to follow the ideology which they barely understood. Jealous neighbors always pointed out the direction for the Red Guards with unfounded rumours. Fancy looking for a human body in a doctor's garden, these are people who had been saving lives for many generations. The doctor's father, who soon succumbed to his injuries, was famed for his skill to treat gun wounds in a chaotic warlord-ruled China before communism arrived. He helped many of his patients with bullet injuries who dared not to go for hospital treatment for various reasons.

No teenagers in anywhere else of our world had as much fun as the youngsters of the Chinese Cultural Revolution generation. They toured the country free by train, they denounced their teachers and attacked anyone at their free will all while there was no classroom and exams to bother them. Then they became the biggest headache for the Chinese authorities, with no university to enter and no jobs to employ them. Finally, one day, all teenagers were asked to get re-educated by factory workers, country farmers or army soldiers for two years as the precondition for those intending to enter university in the future or as permanent employment for the rest. Since joining the army is for the privileged few only, in order to escape the poor farming, everyone wanted to remain in the city with a job in the factory.

That was exactly what my parents persuaded the authorities to do. An impressive achievement for two non-Mandarin speaking, old-fashioned Uyghurs, and with very politically incorrect arguments by current standards. They convinced the teacher, who was one of the army of educators turned into persuaders, that Ibrahim should remain in the city so to continue eating his halal meals at home and marry an Uyghur girl. "Never a Han Chinese girl", they emphasized. Probably the good old days were also sinless days; in the present intolerant climate my parents would either be found guilty as racists in the West or sent to jail as nationalists in China. The modern-day world is not only filled with fake news; everyone has to put out a fake front too.

Ibrahim wasn't gratified that my parents got him a dream job all Chinese teenagers wanted at that era. It wasn't mechanical skills he developed in the factory, he carried on dating girls and spent all his time and money with them going to restaurants.

To do that he had to skip his work regularly the way he played school truancy in the past, but the cheating was conducted tactfully with the help of his very supportive colleagues. In the not-so productive culturally revolutionary China, Ibrahim was able to sign in for work daily by his equally idle colleagues. He signed in for them as well occasionally when they were in need and he was around. This practice was only halted years later when Ibrahim's best friend was unexpectedly killed in a car accident, the bosses were then shocked to discover from the records that the dead man was still working a week after his death.

Ibrahim also made some useful friends in the factory, like the electrician Xiao Guo who was always there to solve our electricity-related household problems. Once Xiao Guo brought in some desperately needed electric cables and refused to accept father's payment. Subsequent communication offended Xiao Guo, as Father advised him to never steal again. Xiao Guo furiously asked me to tell Father to stop calling him a thief. 'I didn't steal the cable, I only took it from my factory' he indignantly declared his innocence. He was right, it was a time when no one worked in the factory and there was no need to check what was produced or missing. Actually everything was up for grabs in the premises. Sometimes you can't even blame the workers as the shops were empty. Xiao Guo, like everyone else, righteously thought he was entitled to take anything he needed to deal with daily problems in life. If the state only offered employees peanuts by pretending people were on the payroll, then they could not complain about the creative way workers subsidized themselves while pretending they were also working.

My parents' high expectations for Ibrahim faded by the time he reached the age of twenty, since their attempts to help Ibrahim to gain some skills or knowledge all but failed. Once they even got an apprenticeship to get Ibrahim interested in dentistry with our highly regarded Polish dentist; it also came to nothing. Woskevicz was a good-natured and hard-working dentist. He took good care of our oral health when it was impossible to get an appointment from the state hospital, but Ibrahim refused to peer into patients' mouths. After two years Ibrahim only managed to produce a couple of metal crowns. I hope they fitted someone's badly decayed teeth after plenty of fillings. Bitterly disappointed and worried sick with the many girls Ibrahim went out with, my parents advised him to get married at the age of 23 and that was when my sister-in-law, Heliqe, joined our family from Shanghai.

There were about ten Uyghur families in Shanghai at that time, all are businessmen's descendants. As the economical hub and the light industrial capital of China, Shanghai was the place to produce and sell all the daily products we need, from clothes to nail clippers. Uyghur businessmen always went there to buy then sold everything back at home. Most of the Uyghurs there were from Atush, the Yorkshire equivalent in Xinjiang. Atush produced the most industrious and shrewd Uyghur businessmen; as a result people from Atush traveled a lot. I am the first Uyghur who came to study in London, and the joke circulated at that time was that there was only one Uyghur in the UK and she is from Atush too. The truth is that my parents were from Atush, I was born in Ghulja. A northern Uyghur city bordering Kazakhstan.

Heliqe was a typical Uyghur beauty. With her long curly hair, big brown eyes, ivory skin and willowy frame, she stood out in any crowd like a film star. A film director even came to ask Heliqe to appear in his film. He needed someone with a Westerner's look to waltz on the dance floor in one of the scenes. Heliqe refused to go since Ibrahim wasn't invited. Years after Ibrahim's marriage, a famous singer I never met before gasped about Heliqe's beauty. 'How you got to know my sister-in-law?' I asked curiously. I was told that half of the residents in Harbin talked about beautiful Heliqe admiringly when she made her first entrance into the city. I assume her large eyes, bushy eyebrows and eyelashes must be highly sought-after features for the Han Chinese, or are they always obsessed with Uyghur beauties?

Iparhan was captured when she was fighting the Qing Dynasty invasion along her father and brother (Han Chinese called her Xiang Fei, which means *fragrant concubine*). She was taken to Beijing and the Qianlong Emperor was captivated by her beauty. It was rumored that her body produced a natural fragrance, and it might just be from a homemade perfume gathered from local blooms. She was a formidable warrior on battlefield as well as in the Forbidden City. She refused to become the emperor's consort, and spent days reclusively looking out of the window like a caged bird. The emperor created an Uyghur-fashioned street in Beijing to please her (which is still there today). He even brought the jujube tree with yellow dates as Iparhan described the golden fruit tree she was missing. When the emperor went hunting, the Dowager asked her to submit herself to the emperor or commit suicide. Heroically she had chosen not to join the enemies she couldn't defeat. After sacrificing her life, her body was transported back to Kashgar Appak Goja mosque for burial.

The portrait of Iparhan was always presented a look of the Han Chinese woman, understandably, as the artists were all Han Chinese and none of them ever had a glance of her. But for her to stand out in a Harem among three thousand concubines, I assume she was young Heliqe alike, an exotic, elegant Uyghur girl. Life in the palace was miserable for the pretty consorts - after being forcefully separated from their families, most of them never even had a chance to meet the emperor who ended up spending his time with a few favorites. As a consequence, it wasn't uncommon for the cursed beauties to put in their entire life hoping and dreaming for the impossible, and some even being savagely buried alive to accompany the dead emperors in their tombs.

There was a one-off happy ending too. A brainy consort volunteered to become the wife of a Mongolian king when given the choice. Instead of sitting there desolately waiting to be noticed, she decided to join her attainable prince and was able to live happily ever after in stunning Mongolia surrounded by horses grazing in the endless green grassland. The rumour was that upon seeing her the emperor wanted to keep this somehow neglected stunner for himself, until the aides reminded the legally philandering emperor about the thousand of beauties like her in Harem (it is called *backyard palace* in Chinese) on standby for his calling. The bride of the Mongolian king brought a decade of truce between the two countries and even enabled the claim that their Mongolian son-in-law was governing Chinese land.

The famous Tibetan Wencheng princess, who was married to the Han Chinese prince, was the other example of Chinese territorial claim from nuptials. Princess Wenchen was a rare beauty; princes from seven neighboring states came to propose to her. Spoilt by choice, the Tibetan King set out many riddles for the princes to solve. One last hurdle featured the princess being joined by another seven Tibetan girls in a beauty identity parade. The clever Han Chinese prince discovered from a maid about Wencheng princess's love of wildflowers, so he befittingly identified the princess when he saw bees were circling around her. According to the legend the princess introduced butter and cheese to China, but it didn't seem to take off among the Han Chinese. Butter and cheese are still only Uyghur, Mongolian and Tibetan's staple diet.

Ibrahim's marriage lasted forever. On his deathbed my sister-in-law sobbed her heart out once he stopped breathing. Like all married couples, they had their ups and downs during their 46 years of marriage, but the relationship survived since they never stopped loving each other. So much went bitterly wrong in Ibrahim's career: a failed mechanic, a futile effort in a long dentistry apprenticeship, an unaccomplished businessman but he was a caring husband and devoted father beyond doubt. He brought up three hard-working sons in an estate notoriously resided by many drug dealers. He took his children to school in the morning and collected them after school to keep them out of trouble. A heavy drinker himself and a chain smoker too, he made sure none of his children ever touched any of these toxic substances. None of his handsome sons even had a chance to become another young Casanova under Ibrahim's watchful eyes. Sometimes it makes me wonder if a sinful past is the perfect recipe for a successful fatherhood.

Ibrahim had a stroke at the age of sixty. Years of indulgence in food, drink and cigarettes finally clogged his arteries and created blood clots in his brain. He survived the stroke after two brain operations in the hospital and spent four months in intensive care. He made no progress there and doctors were puzzled by his regular fever. When the money from the flat we sold had run out (hence his youngest son had to move back to his parents' home), we made the heartbreaking decision to care for his last days at home. Two weeks after Ibrahim came back home, it became clear that the weekly visit by the nurse gave him the fever, apparently from the injection to keep the cannula unblocked. We decisively removed the cannula from his wrist and that put an end to the contaminated fluid entering Ibrahim's body again. The weekly feverish torture was finally over, replaced with significant progress. Gradually he started eating himself without the feeding tube and thankfully talking too.

Not many people in the West are aware of the fact that Communist China only provide free health care for government officials. People who work in private sectors, and particularly those unfortunately unemployed, had to pay their own medical bill. They might have to borrow money or sell their residency like we did. When my aunt lost her consciousness, the ambulance took her to hospital and straight to the theater while her family waited outside. Halfway while the doctors were still trying to save my aunt's life, the nurse came out to tell her husband that the money they paid was used up and more payment was required for further treatment. It was horrifying to hear that my aunt would be kept alive only if they had money. My sister, who was telling me the story for an entirely different reason, tried to assure me it wasn't the case. Then why not settle the bill after the emergency is over? Her husband paid anyway. Sadly, my aunt never regained her consciousness and her life support was switched off a month later when the medical bill grew too big to sustain. It was the year 2009, my aunt was 72 years old.

Jung Chang's family misfortune in *Wild Swan* is heart breaking to read. Her staunchly loyal father worked in provincial and later state propaganda department to glorify the communist regime. Yet he died young as an anti-revolutionist. However, she revealed little about the numerous privileges her family enjoyed until the Cultural Revolution struck. As the daughter of two high ranking government officers, Jung Chang must be brought up in a rent-free house with free medical care and even servants, called *Ayi*. When her mother spent three months in the hospital, there were no financial worries to compound their problem. Since she only rubbed shoulders with *Gaogan zidi*, the Princelings of the communist official in high places, she certainly was oblivious of ordinary folks' suffering.

During the great Chinese famine of 1960s, a starving colleague of mine went to meet his powerful future mother-in-law for lunch. With her never-shrinking, larger than life frame, the head of women's affairs in Xinjiang ordered a meal for my colleague in the canteen only catered for people in high positions. After rapidly swallowing every bit of his own share to fill his empty stomach, my colleague went round the canteen tables to collect all the leftovers. What he didn't expect was the horrified look on other diners' faces, as the privileged lot didn't even know that his ravenously hungry classmates were looking forward to feast on the promised leftovers. China is the nest of nepotism - you can find more equality in the caste system of India.

Nine years after his stroke, my optimistic sister and sister-in-law took Ibrahim to Turfan to celebrate Eid. It was two weeks after his 69th birthday and his first holiday since he lost control of half his body. On his third day he died of a suspected heart attack there. Just like my father, his heart stopped beating before the ambulance could reach him. Maybe they forgot his blood pressure tablets or gave him too much kebab from the newly slaughtered big, fat mutton. His heart unexpectedly failed to cope anymore. The last time I talked to him was on our double birthday, then I couldn't reach him during that Eid. I decided to call him the next day, and cruelly life froze for him on that day with no more tomorrows to follow.

CHAPTER 4 KEMAL

If only you can come back for one more day,
I long to see your smile and handsome face;
please fill the house with your humour and
laughter, instead of leaving me to suffer in
this empty gutter.

This was the first time in my life I had witnessed the scene of death unfold before me. To have a send off surrounded by his loved ones in his leisurely domestic setting was the wish of my husband, but I look back at it with so much gravity instead of ease. Only in hindsight did it become evident to me that I had unwittingly rushed my husband out of the world a few hours earlier than he should have, all while I was trying too hard to relieve his pain.

I was having the recurring nightmare which has terrified me all my life: the sky has fallen on me while I was walking. I think the reason for the torment by sky fall started on a heavy rainy night, a piece of plaster landed on my face from the crumbing ceiling in my bedroom, I must have been five then. The ceiling was fixed by the builder the next day, but fifty-eight years on, the most disturbing nightmare in many different forms has never ceased to disturb me.

It was Boxing Day morning 2018. I woke from the same frightening nightmare with sweat. The fact that my husband Kemal, the man I trusted the most in my life was with me when the sky descended didn't make me feel safe. With my eyes still closed I started soul-searching: how come his presence failed to calm me? Then reality suddenly hit me: Kemal was cancer-stricken and resting on a borrowed hospital bed next to me. I jumped out of the sofa and grabbed his hands while he was asleep with an endearing smile.

Now I could recall the horror. Until three hours ago, Kemal was in so much pain, he requested, "Do something about it!". The power of morphine I administered earlier was gone, now he needed more. Feeling immensely guilty for leaving him to endure this unbearable pain, and with unsteady hands, I injected twice the previous dose of morphine. My heart never ached so much as I helplessly stared at him clenching his teeth together, simultaneously twisting his body to cope with the excruciating pain. It felt like it took forever for the drug to kick in, then finally he stopped groaning deeply. The last question he asked me before the medication took effect was about the morphine dosage. 'Ten mil,' I answered. He nodded. Even when death was so close and pain so severe, Kemal still remembered to show his usual appreciation. 'Good,' he added. It was 3:45 am.

I sat down on the sofa and watched him slowly closed his eyes without ever blinking my own. Satisfied to see him finally pain-free, I slowly drifted away to rest my anxiety-ridden brain. Two weeks ago, Kemal was discharged from St Bartholomew's Hospital for palliative care at home. I was over the moon to be with him all day, he was pleased to reclaim the delightful feeling of liberty at home. However, the exhaustion and sleep deprivation made me constantly pass out on the sofa next to his bed.

Now, at quarter to seven, I stood there quietly staring at his handsome face. Kemal looked divine for some reason; an overspread smile gave the impression that he was indulged in a sweet dream. I bent down to kiss him, but to my horror he didn't seem to be breathing. All of a sudden, I felt a shiver down my spine. Was the impression on his face a permanent one? Had my husband left me during the quiet, small hours of the morning? I placed my shaking hands on his chest; there was no heartbeat either.

The next few hours, few days, few months even a year went on like a blur, with no chance for me to engage in any meaningful mourning. All I can recall now was an ambulance arrived first, then came the police. They left in reverse order, first the police after the paramedics informed them that the death was a natural one, then the ambulance left as soon as I delivered Kemal's Do Not Resuscitate message.

The undertakers came. They turned Kemal over and black bile flew out of his mouth. With a quick wipe, they swiftly zipped him up into the leather body bag and rushed out of the door. 'No' I attempted to scream and stop them from taking my husband away in such a manner. Sadly, a lump appeared in my throat and took away the words about to come out from my lips. Desperately I waited for Kemal to respond, usually the clean freak him would protest and demand a thorough cleaning. Of course, he didn't. What is death but a ghostly silence! Darkness engulfed me as the true nature of death unveiled itself. From this moment on, Kemal's opinion does not count anymore, since the world has moved on without his existence already. Death is a million times worse than I have ever imagined.

A GP arrived before the undertakers to issue the letter for the death certificate. I told her that Kemal was also a GP who did his part in helping thousands of people during his 49 year-long medical career. 'So he was a great man then', said the GP, she continued. 'How wonderful for you to inform me about a fruitful life with high achievement'. She added, 'I often walk into a house with lonely, dead old people I knew nothing about. There was no one to tell me anything of the deceased'.

Could that be Kemal had we not met? He was 45 when 32-year-old me walked into his life. As someone who had been cautious about committing himself, he uncharacteristically proposed to me. The reason seemed because I was this least conventional female companion Kemal had ever met in his life, while all his previous girlfriends had already blended into one unrecognizable body. Our two beautiful daughters often remind us what a blessing that we met. We continued our life journey together to be true to our destiny. The dreamy 31 years had gone by like a flash, with highlights to inform us it was not only yesterday that we wed. We could have blissfully spent another 31 years together, had we been granted with such everlasting luck. The curse finally struck with one of us being cruelly taken away to a far away land.

I was probably twelve when I was reading *The Brothers Yershov* by Russian writer Vsevelod Kochetov. When the Yershov brothers lost their mother, who died tragically in her 30s, they were not half as sad as their father for the great loss. Kochetov's interpretation for the emotional state of father was that the light in his life was turned off while his sons' light had yet to be turned on. Confused, I asked my parents: "How could the father's future be pitch dark when he still had his sons?". Mother pointed out to me that the father had lost the one person who meant the most to him in his life; Father nodded approvingly at the same time.

Like many egocentric teenagers, my self-glorification was dealt the first severe blow. Until that point, I always thought of myself as the most important person to my parents. After all, they openly doted on me whereas my other siblings had been less favoured. Mercifully, my perspective was far from the truth: my parents never cared about my siblings less, it was just they worried about my over-sensitivity more. It is no coincidence for parents to offer preferential treatment for their over and above delicate, weepy poor little souls like me. I know it as a mother myself now and realised that my siblings view their deficiently received attention as a necessary protection of me in disguise. Finally, I further go along with my parents' conclusion that my two daughters make life worth living, but the harsh reality is that my light has gone out with Kemal. Without his acquired insight into my character, I live in a dim world surrounded by murky understanding.

We all enter marriage with eyes wide open, while not consciously aware that we are about to live under the impact of a most received companion. By the time I noticed Kemal's unmistakable influence on me, he already absorbed my whole soul, then moulded it into almost the same shape as his. As a result I matured into a more thoughtful and patient person compared to the one with a less mellow personality from my salad days. To a lesser extent, Kemal could have said the same about me, since I had managed to alter a few of his worldviews too. In terms of our life we took our chance seriously, i.e. carved out a happy life for the four of us in the family while transforming each other during the process.

If meeting Kemal was a predestined blessing, then marrying him certainly gave rise to serendipity. We had been husband and wife, soulmates and most importantly mentors for each other. There is so much to learn in life, especially if the two of you are from such different backgrounds. He hailed from a town called Nigde of central Turkiye, I was born in Xinjiang then brought up in Harbin of Chinese Manchuria. In 1970, Kemal decided to come to the UK to further his medical career after he completed his medical degree in Istanbul University; in 1984 I obtained a grant to do my master's degree in Imperial College. In London we met, and the rest is history.

From such a distinctive background, I used to narrate the strangest facts from Central Asia to

Kemal. It came as a huge surprise for Kemal, a medical doctor, to know that hospitals arrived so late for Uyghurs, only folk medicine and midwives were present to deal with all types of medical issues as well as childbirth for centuries. In 1984, a Swedish woman found me in Montpellier Student Hall during my Imperial College years; she claimed her father opened a hospital in Kashgar in the 1930s. Her mother, who worked as a nurse, was in her 80s when we met in a London hotel. She hugged me with tears in her eyes. I felt I knew her all along, the Mother Teresa of the Uyghur nation.

I was surprised that my courteous parents never mentioned the kindness of this Swedish family to me. How could one not feel grateful for their ultimate sacrifice? After all, they swapped the comfort of Sweden for the harsh reality in Kashgar, not to mention the lives they had saved. My deeply religious father's answer to my query was to deny that these people were Swedish medics, he insisted that things were not as they seemed. He further claimed that the family I met were Christian missionaries with a hidden agenda.

It was a pity that Father never made an effort to know these people as he was also in Kashgar during the 1930s, and relied on hearsay which he narrated with the intention to convince me. However, meeting this extraordinary nurse who assisted her doctor husband helping the Kashgaris pierced my heart. I couldn't shrug off the inherent connection between us. I still could feel the warmth from her hug, recalling the tears she shed. I admire her courage, a Western woman whose heart spoke the same language like Uyghurs. I don't even believe the patients they treated and saved were required to trade their Islamic belief for Christianity. Kemal agreed with me, I just wish I was able to convince Father too.

I can't say it took me 32 years to find the life companion for myself, since we are all contented in the first and a half decades of our lives to remain in an environment filled with people we share many strands of DNA with. It must be from that age I started consciously searching for a man, not to sail to the sunset with him one day, but to roam the wide world first then move ahead towards our life journey together. Maybe it is a female thing to give marriage so much thought, as I am well aware the world is not short of men living in fear of commitment, while the girls lead the parade for domestication with all their might.

With such a mindset, I even rushed into a wrong marriage, then equally quickly got out of it. It was worse than being imprisoned to live with someone so incompatible. The fact that my first marriage was like a black society which only I knew how dark it was didn't stop me from entering into the second one. With the unpleasant taste of the bitter pill from the failed nuptials still present, I fell head over heels in love with Kemal soon after we met. By the time we tied the knot after spending a good four years getting to know each other, I was absolutely sure he was the one. It is strange to think that I had to travel such a distance to find a man that I can live under the same roof harmoniously with contentment. Holding fast to my dream to enter a matrimony in love allowed me to live happily ever after, that includes present day life with my mind reaching to Kemal at a celestial sphere while rooted on the ground for our daughters.

Life becomes less challenging when one navigates in the world with a friend together. The gates of happiness remain open for friends, even more so for those who set blazing flames on their friendship with love and subsequently end up being lifetime companions. Suddenly I found myself calling Kemal my other half since I felt so complete for the first time ever in my life. I loved pursuing ideas for two, I enjoyed the endless discussions with him. Those debates, at times heated, gave birth to many brilliant ideas and stimulated later observations. I miss the days decisions were made jointly; now I have to shoulder all the burden and frequently worry about the consequences. Not that Kemal's views are discarded, I still go after the options closest to his heart.

Being a medical doctor is the most fitting job for a man with devotion like Kemal, it enabled him to quench his sole desire to help people and save lives. Apart from his intelligence, hard work and resourcefulness, what made Kemal stand out from the rest of the herd was his compassion and kindness. I didn't think much of a GP's functionality until I met him. Working alongside Kemal enabled me to understand the complexity of GP's duty and what a valuable medical service they offer. I am impressed with his dedication to his patients' welfare; Kemal's tireless work in prevention and consequently timely detection of severe health problems from his patients must have saved many lives.

I know the surgeons are the superstars of our time, and everyone is in awe of their life-saving skills and power. When my sister's friend suffered from oral cancer in the early 1970s, the overwhelmed surgeon in Harbin suggested to remove the tumour on her gum, including part of her face. Fortunately, the young woman was destined to survive with a better outcome. She went to Beijing where an experienced surgeon managed to cut out the cancer cells without disfiguring her. It was such a pleasure to see her emerge from surgery in her original form and go on to live a healthy and happy life for decades to come. She gave birth to a healthy baby son two years later.

But surgery is a body mending process while preventative measures take place continuously long before that in GP consultation room. The right health advice and the timely detection as well as referral is the way to save precious lives, sometimes without medical procedures. That is essentially what primary care is all about and the root of Kemal's pride and joy. As a GP, Kemal's whole existence was centered towards his patients' needs, it was the source for his passionate devotion. With all that warmth within him, Kemal always listened to his patients' concerns carefully. No shortage of wonders from his treatments, he delighted his patients with the right diagnosis time after time. No challenges were too big and no illnesses were too trivial for Kemal to treat. His persistence and his desire to care for others enabled him to be immensely resourceful.

One morning our daughter's school teacher arrived with a severe stomach ache. He crouched while clutching his lower body in agony and bit his lower lip to quell the groan from his excruciating pain. Kemal helped the teacher into his consultation room. Fifteen minutes later when I went down to check if the ambulance was called, much to my pleased astonishment the smiling teacher sat comfortably in his seat and chatting to Kemal. Apparently Kemal gave him an injection to soothe his hurting, that tranquilizing effect was able to assist him to pass the bladder stone out. An amazing even magical solution! Kemal's valuable expertise saved the teacher from a painful trip to A&E. With long queues, no quick fix there as we all know.

With a strong desire to help, Kemal was eager to expend further time and effort to make sure his patients get the best care. A lonely female patient interpreted Kemal's readiness to go the extra mile to assist as an interest in herself and when he made it clear that she was just one of his patients, she furiously filed a complaint. Due to the incompetence of prosecution (the case was incidentally assigned to a WPC on maternity leave), then the over-enthusiastic yet thoroughly incompetent customer service officer from the local authorities (who persuaded the patient not to drop her complaint by heaping praise on her 'bravery'), the case unnecessarily ended up in the crown prosecution court.

After listening to the plaintiff's very unconvincing narratives, the judge ordered jury to quit Kemal even without the need for him to be cross examined. I was shocked to witness the taxpayers' money could be wasted in such a manner. It was impossible not to fume with rage, seeing the reckless culprit who started all these false accusations walked out of court unpunished and unrepentant, moaning about 'unfair British justice'.

It was the most stressful time of our life, while waiting for more than a year to start the court action intensified our anguish. Unbelievably the patient who initiated the legal process doggedly refused to attend the court in the summer as the date supposedly clashed with her holiday arrangement. Finally the trial was agreed for December when I was heavily pregnant. The only silver lining out of the legal proceeding was to have the honour to meet Anthony Arlidge, QC, the barrister who the Medical Defense Union appointed to defend Kemal. Unlike the lawyers in *LA Law* from TV, I found Mr. Anthony Arlidge had a delightfully mild British manner, not at all aggressive or antagonizing like his American counterparts. Yet he hit the point every time, in spite of kindly offering the plaintiff ample time to compose her answers. Despite my lingering worries about the final verdict, I found the entire process reassuring, even enjoyable. Never had I imagined to witness a top legal brain exposed fantasies and lies with the compelling evidence in a court room.

After observing such a fine brilliant barrister and knowing he was involved in some truly famous cases, I expected to find Mr. Arlidge's name on some national newspaper or honour list after the court proceedings. Finally in 2005 I found he secured the acquittal for Dr. Hayward Martin from his murder trial. I had to dig through the text which reported the story to find his name printed twice only. His newsworthy moment arrived in 2012 on Daily Mail. It was not about his meticulous work, now 75-years old, he left his partner of twenty years for a young lawyer. Seeing this great man's wonderful work being overlooked, while his private life splashed out on papers for gossipers to enjoy broke my heart. Kemal also felt sad that people were not informed about Mr. Arlidge's hard work, kindness and dedication in saving reputations as well as lives of many decent doctors. After all he was part of the legal team in prosecution of Jeremy Bamber's case; I was also told that he even played a part in defending Birmingham six to overturn the guilty verdict.

Kemal burst into tears when he was acquitted. Mr. Arlidge kindly remarked about his pleasure to see Kemal came out from the court without any stain. All I did was trying hard not to cry. It was difficult to go through an unnecessary trial. Had the accuser been persuasive in her lies, Kemal could have been made guilty and would have lost his job. I know for sure that his life would be non-existent without his medical profession. This unpleasant event happened to be in the early 90s, a time when the internet was mercifully absent and no ominous social media to complicate matters or to terminate our final hope. These days internet trolls or GP haters would undermine the legal process by claiming no smoke without fire. It is not unusual to see utterly innocent people tried by social media, and being plunged into the realm of darkness and despair by collective outrage.

In fact there were plenty fun aspects from Kemal's profession too. During one of his night visits from his deputizing work, Kemal met Wayne Rooney's grandparents. The elderly couple were exceedingly proud of their 17-year old grandson, who already was a premiership footballer. Soon we found out that Wayne Rooney was transferred to Manchester United from Everton football club, and even started counting his endless scores. By the end of the year, we were pleased to see him named BBC's Young Sports Personality Of The Year 2002. The bond with Kemal's patients has elevated Wayne Rooney to the position of our favourite legendary footballer despite both of us being Arsenal supporters. Watching him play for England in many World Cups made us proud too, only wish we had won it at least once.

New Year's Day on 2019 was my unhappiest ever, the day I buried Kemal in Kilyos, a cemetery in outskirts of Istanbul. Since then I have visited Kemal many times already. I love the peace his cemetery offers me. The calm atmosphere here gives me a chance to enjoy the beauty of nature and its wonderful serenity. The tall pine trees which encircles Kemal's tomb enchanted my aching heart with its splendour. The thought of Kemal being guarded by spirits had temporarily allowed me not to grieve the lack of his full existence. I am aware of Kemal's fondness of this place too, since that was what he told me after burying his mother fourteen years ago. Yet the dream to buy the next plot was shattered by someone else's swifter action. We could only get hold of the spot one grave further away from where my mother-in-law was put to rest.

While I am casting a loving look on Kemal's grave, there was no escaping from the settled ones who are sandwiched between our family members. The man was buried there one day after my mother-in-law's funeral, and he is not alone either, a woman is resting next to him who must be his wife. What a surprise for me to discover that she died just one day after Kemal, before the end of 2018. My mother-in-law was 83 when she left this world, while Kemal was 76. I turned towards the couples' grave, and my heart sank even further to discover that they perished so much younger than my loved ones: the husband was only 40 and wife was 54 years old. Four of them, the earthlings of this planet, not aware of each other's destiny, now all left the hazy world then swallowed by this vast earth on the same spot.

Other people's more tragic lives may sadden me,

but some others left me with plenty of envy too. A man nursed his father back to health after the hospital sent him back home to die from coronavirus. Now his father is virus-free. While I couldn't even ease Kemal's pain of his cancer wrecked body.

So here I am, in the only spot Kemal still occupies on this planet. I would sit alone there staring at his tombstone and quietly blame myself for not being able to save him. Deep in his sleep, silent forever, Kemal would not know that I was there with him. No need to reach out for the sleeping tablets anymore, all of a sudden a simplified life on earth has become Kemal's regular existence beneath the ground. Staring at his resting place, I want to tell him that I did imagine his departure one day after he was diagnosed with cancer, but when that nightmare isn't a vision anymore, I realized those thoughts do not even come close to reality. Now I am haunted by not enjoying my life in full during our heavenly marriage. Beware that life is about relishing the moment and not to dwell too much on the uncertain, unavoidable and unalterable future.

Trying to come to terms with his death made me revisit the night Kemal perished so often, I can almost recall the scenes minute by minute. He was calm and resigned, not loading us with advice, not demanding any promises and not even expressing his worries for our future life without him. That is the type of modest person Kemal always was, no sense of entitlement to indispensability. I do hope in his heavenly thoughts he felt that all topics were covered with me already, since we had endless conversations during our lives together. No topic was off limits. When his end drew near, Kemal might be comforted with the thought that nothing was left unsaid on his deathbed. Could the satisfaction that all was said and would be done had made death more tolerable?

One topic Kemal spent years discussing with me is about Uyghur independence, an eternally non-negotiable issue from the Han Chinese point of view. Under colonial orders, the Uyghur nation is notified to remain dutifully under Chinese state tutelage with no alternative to ponder. The authorities also grace and adorn our coexistence with idiosyncratic rhetoric such as *minorities can't live without the Han Chinese, and the Han Chinese can't live without the minorities.* Lofty slogans like this was weaponized in China to reflect their strategic focus long before they innocently appeared on T-shirts in the West. At any rate the authorities can sound persuasively charming with their intension to create a *harmonious society*, which in reality embodies the essence of totalitarian doctrine: to contrive a China with even less choice by cracking down on freedom of speech.

Though the Han Chinese do come to depend critically on the land of Uyghurs, Tibetans and Mongolians, it never has stopped them to inanely see us as the *less evolved ethnic groups*. Nevertheless we happen to make up sixty percent of Chinese territory with rich natural resources, and where these days millions of Han Chinese reside and are still emigrating. But if the Chinese think we can't live without their technology, they had better think again. The question of a rather delicate nature here is do we want to live with the ecological consequences caused by the Han Chinese settlement in our land, or manage our own natural resources sustainably and reverse the environmental damage independently.

In 1954, the Xinjiang Production and Construction Corps were set up to cultivate and defend our frontiers with military personnel. They boasted about their policy not competing with the benefits of local people and declared their intention to develop a new settlement for the Han Chinese in the *hopeless fertility* of the Taklimakan Desert. Yet the so called amazing towns and cities were built over the open pastures near Urumqi with deplorable consequences. This ended the green beauty of our land, left sheep with no grassland to graze, not to mention also making Urumqi more prone to natural disasters. However it did help to bring in millions of Han Chinese to

Xinjiang from the *enclave of the great wall of China* (that is the Uyghur name for the Han Chinese homeland).

However, fighting the Chinese for our independence will be a David and Goliath situation, just without the possibility of a wining outcome for the underdog. No one can attempt to wage a war against the Chinese without being broken by them. Fighting to our last breath could possibly become a genocidal total wipeout of the Uyghur nation. A super nuclear power state like China can't be defeated with guerrilla warfare. Not to forget the enemy in front of us, the Chinese Liberation Army is the biggest state military force in the world, highly experienced too.

To complicate matters, there is also a very scary enemy behind us. Xinjiang is effectively the Chinese Siberia, with tens and thousands, probably millions of the most dangerous Han Chinese criminals from all parts of China on exile there. Once let loose, these violent villains inevitably would cause the most horrendous bodily and psychological harm to the Uyghur nation, even setting off cluster bombs could be considered tame or kind by comparison. No sane nation would go through this type of grievous risk to pursue a brand-new state, even on the basis to protect our diminishing culture.

With all the pejorative overtones of the word

colonialism, I used to blame all our problems on the lack of independence. My nationalist dream is to live independently ever after with an ignited faith on a definite happy ending. Now I am fully aware that my hopes for independence may amount to nothing more than a sublime work of fiction, and only in fiction one can live happily ever after. The downward trajectory of independence may well turn self-determination into the beginning of many more new nightmares. The concept of independence itself is a dated delusional goal, long lost its appeal in the last 50 years. When the most powerful country in the world is 51 states united to one, and the next successful union is formed by 27 independent European nations, you know there is life beyond independence.

Furthermore, the concept of independence alone is not enough for survival. To start from scratch and reinventing the wheel, then open up embassies the world over is an illusion. Besides, independence is not food, it doesn't offer the homeless any shelter and doesn't provide business opportunities either. No nation can ever be truly independent sandwiched between China and Russia, the two gigantic remaining empires of our time. The independent Central Asian republics are still all under Russian spell, while China treats all their neighbours as one of their provinces, bar India. It is a geographical curse laid upon us. If we haven't already belonged to one of them, then we will end up being dominated by the other regional bully.

Even if independence is achieved through a gentle process, there are till many calamities to overcome. The one outcome I loathe the most is that social uprising almost always being hijacked and ultimately ruined by power hungry individuals. These opportunists have no interest in independence, freedom, national identity or the creation of a more affluent society. They are addicted to power, and crave the chance to enter the world stage to rub shoulders with other world leaders. A lot of the leaders of newly independent states are dictators, or the type who becomes corrosive the moment they get near to power. I am holding out hope that no young Uyghur men and women's precious lives will be wasted to put some selfish weirdo in a powerful position. Once the feverish desire for self-determination has faded into obscurity, those who lost loved ones will be left to lick their own wounds. Don't expect any support from the sleazily crowned new callous government, since the tyranny might be the replica of what he has just replaced. The self-governing dream could be marred with the creation of a belligerent state without fairness.

War should be avoided at all costs since we all know it is destructively a recipe for disaster.

Besides the aftermath of war can easily derail the peace process and initiate new fights. That is what exactly has happened in Afghanistan and Iraq. When America, the self-appointed protector of *international democracy,* declared their mission accomplished during early 2000s, the war-torn Afghanistan and Iraq descended into more chaos. Despite the efforts to sustain the peace, more bloodshed became the means to settle the ancient scores. The never ending conflict turned the counting of the dead bodies into a daily routine in those ill-fated countries. Many families have not only lost their loved ones, they also became the internally displaced refugees permanently, unable to return to where they belong to. War never solves problems, it creates new predicaments like welcoming Taliban 2.0 after twenty years' bloodshed. America can absent itself from trouble with abrupt departure, but the Afghans can't.

Watching the Afghan boy falling off the airplane to America reminded me of the story I read about the chaotic time as the Qing Dynasty collapsed in China. In the sorrowful tale, Xu Dishan recorded on the eve when the Han Chinese regained power, people were shouting in the street to kill all Manchurians. Though it was to no one in particular, a panic-stricken Manchurian officer who served the Qing Emperor decided to assassinate his own family to escape the forthcoming torture. He stabbed his wife and two sons but failed to find his little daughter, who escaped the onslaught hiding in a tree. In the morning peace the little girl came down the tree to find her mother and brothers' bodies with two severed fingers on the floor. The girl was familiar with those fingers from her father as she used to stroke them playfully. Now with a mission to find her father, she joined the circus, she would stare at the crowd while performing on the high wire with the hopes of finding him. On a boat trip she accidentally knocked down a mobile gas stove, it was a monk who saved everyone on the boat by extinguishing the fire with his own body. Holding the dying monk, the devastated girl found out that two fingers were missing from his left hand.

In 1975 the euphoria of defeating America in Vietnam was replaced by the widespread despair with the total collapse of the economy. Desperate to find a way out, Vietnam turned to China once more, expecting their saviour to wave the magic wand again. In no ambiguous terms Chairman Mao, a towering political figure with profound influence of his own time, instructed Vietnamese leaders to start rebuilding their country by mercilessly purging all those who collaborated with Americans. Mao also harboured hatred towards intellectuals, he asked the Vietnamese to put them on their hit list too. Vietnam hesitated, then turned their back to China.

Arrived fresh, the Cambodian government (crowned with Chinese assistance, of course) decided to follow the ill-fated advice unmitigatedly, the ultimate death and destruction even exceeded the ambitious goal their pushy mentor set up for them. The killing fields in Cambodia was the result of extracting the penalties from many who were suspected of connections with the former regime. The professionals also borne the blame, being executed or starved to death during the process of apportionment. By carrying the punishment practice to excess, the regime survived without further challenge, but over millions of dead bodies. We have suffered enough to never repeat the sordid history of *killing field* in our era, on our land.

The town at the lower stream of the Songhua River has a Japanese women's cemetery. The women were buried in August 1945 after Japan only evacuated their defeated military personnel. Brought into Manchuria as settlers, these women with children were ruthlessly abandoned to their own fate while Russian soldiers closed in. They waited in vain for Japanese rescue boats. With faded hope, many women just walked into the deathly river to a harrowing end on their own. Local Chinese families adopted the children, some were only infants while the young and single ladies married the Chinese men with grim courage. In Harbin we all had classmates with Japanese mothers without any knowledge of their haunting past. In the late 1970s, the Japanese government finally allowed all their descendants to settle in Japan. One such woman in her 30s repatriated to Japan together with her adoptive Chinese mother whom she loves dearly. Initially she was ecstatic to find her biological mother survived the turbulence and even had a new family of her own now. Sadly the reunion dejected her spirits as it became obvious that she has become the liability of unraveling her Japanese mother's well-hidden *shameful past*. Many war wounds never heal.

As peace-loving as we always are, we Uyghurs, Tibetans and Mongolian are the victims from our inconceivable hospitality. It may seem absurd now that we welcomed the early Han Chinese settlers with open arms, offered them food and shelter, not realising that they had this amazing staying power. Millions more Han Chinese rushed through the unlocked Jade Gate and in the process made us the minority in our own homeland. The sun would have carried on shining on us if the Han Chinese followed the custom of the land they made home rather than glutting their perilous will with instinct and habitude on us. Across the foothold they have gained over our sacred motherland, the effort to make our idyllic home so domineeringly all that is Han Chinese has robbed us from our inalienable rights.

Back in the 1950s, Uyghur education was already established on Russian system with textbooks imported from Uzbekistan. But the policy of Sinicization leaves no room for Uzbek books and Uyghur language was replaced with Mandarin. This served as a catalyst to empower the Han Chinese and left Uyghur students trailing behind in educational hell which produced precisely the sought after effects from the authorities with mass unemployment among non Mandarin speaking *undeveloped* populations. The Han Chinese are blessed to study for a degree using their own tongue, whereas we are left with so many more matters to navigate: to gain professional skills with a linguistically foreign language. Ignoring Uyghur, Tibetan and Mongolian difficulties, Chinese always accuse us for being not as smart as them, or put in other way, just plainly stupid.

Our culture is no less ancient or glorious than the Han Chinese culture, but without the ingredients to take ourselves too seriously. Being instructed to live in Chinese customs has left us helplessly worried that our ancestral tradition may fade and finally vanish in a matter of decades. Instead of abandoning their fiendish policy, Chinese authorities consider their tyrannical grip over us as not robust enough. With a rigid focus on exaggerated danger from the very few toothless separatists, our intellectuals are labelled as terrorists and being locked up. In addition to all the obvious detrimental impact caused to our welfare and survival, many Chinese scientific descriptions and classifications have found their way to replace Uyghur's established narratives. The end result of this wide ramification is our diminished culture and a brief shelf life of less than fifty years for Uyghur language, a perfect fitting for the hellish assimilation plan.

With a philosophy that stresses collective rather than individual rights, no thought is spared for Uyghur speakers' survival. Those who can't get their accents right are among the damned. During a heated argument even my Uyghur colleague's not-so-perfect Chinese accent was being mocked. Maybe because racism and colonialism often come hand-in-hand and you are supposed to despise the people you have defeated, then with the air of self-declared superiority demand a return of obedience from the native. If the triumph of a nation is always supposed to bring in the downfall of another, who could blame us for living in a constant state of fear from the existential threat cast on us!

It was absurd to hear a Han Chinese woman claimed that no good looking Tibetan exists in the world. She insisted the beautiful girl with a glowing Tibetan skin and prominent cheekbones who performed in the Royal Festival Hall was a Chinese in disguise. Sadly, it is a snobbish and vile view shared by many of her kind, as there are a whole lot of them even dreaming of owning the entire Mongolia. This type of *enough requires too much, too much craves more* mentality has served the Han Chinese handsomely. Mongolians sing about their grievous population decline in Inner Mongolia (the independent Mongolia is called outer Mongolia in China) while hopelessly watching their population be reduced to only 10% of the local inhabitants, an inevitable consequence after a century of impeded Han Chinese emigration. Their songs echo their melancholy with compelling pulchritude, accompanied by Morin khuur (their traditional *horse head fiddle,* but only the strings are from horse tail while no horse was harmed during the process of making the instrument).

Though weary in spirit we exact for granting peace ahead. Chinese rulers could surely find a viable way to carve out a common ground for all people in China, so that we can live peacefully side by side in a sensible and mutual-respect promoting society. To inculcate a sense of trust in us a sentient government will start aligning with the needs of Uyghur people too. Instead of locking up our intellectuals who never broke their pact with the authorities, let Uyghurs thrive under our own culture; instead of keeping the Arabic script, teach our Latin script to Uyghur children from primary school days, which was developed with the help of the Han Chinese linguistics. An omnipotent sovereign like China shouldn't be threatened by a few million Uyghurs who are renowned for our love of singing and dancing.

Even with dolorous experience from the past, we can still be united and move on towards our interwoven destiny with empathy and passion. It is futile to dream for the impossible, we Uyghurs overwhelmingly prefer to pursue happiness with the Han Chinese together. It might sound like hope springs in our breast, but with good faith we can lighten up our future by not eliding the abyss between us, but to accept our differences and be each other's dependable partner indulgently. Life isn't about scuttling away to our Central Asian cousins' homeland as refugees under their familiar favour. I have seen the pain of traumatic dislocation, and most Uyghurs will not trade paradise with our beloved homeland, the land of our ancestors.

When the daughter of an army officer fell madly in love with her father's handsome Uyghur bodyguard in 1950, he was ordered to marry her in no uncertain terms. The forced nuptial with a Han Chinese woman instead of his childhood sweetheart unsettled the Uyghur man even after thirty years, having three children together with a pampered existence. He escaped to Kumul, his birthplace as soon as his own son, now an army officer himself, threatened to shoot his father for attempting to divorce his mother. In his adult life, the man was denied the right to live in a simple, traditional Uyghur way with the love of his life. Through a late life dash, he said so long to his stalled misery under imprisonment with admirable bravery. Finally he returned home, to spend his autumn years in the only place he can experience a glimpse of heaven.

Kemal was moved to tears by my story. He despised colonial torment. In his ideal world, one day we may all be able to *untangle* ourselves from the *twist of melancholy* of losing our home and culture. His pacifist poem may have expressively set out a lofty goal for human society, nevertheless might be the only option to real happiness of mankind:

Children of this planet,
This is our promised land;
No shut borders, no famine,
One day New York one day Beijing.
Christian, Buddhist, Judaist, Muslim,
Everlasting peace is our only aim.

Europe, America, Asia, Africa,
Different beliefs, different colours;

It isn't late for salvation,
Same human, all brothers.
Give up weapons so the dove can soar high,
Live in a world waves war its final goodbye.

CHAPTER 5 MOURNING

Now I know how short lived happiness could be, I miss the days you belonged to me; cherished memories of our love keeps you near, the courage you instilled in me chases away my fear.

My first sorrow arrived at the age of 16, when my cat Pasha died. Pasha was only 6 years old, she may have taken ill after catching and consuming a poisoned mouse. After burying her under the apricot tree in the garden with tears blurring my vision, I promised her that I would never smile again. Yet life was back to normal very soon. Summer time when the apricot was ripe, I would guiltily eat the fruit sitting besides Pasha's grave, calling myself a disloyal friend. Actually she never slipped out of my mind. Thirty years on, I wrote a story of Pasha when parents were asked to write down their childhood memories in my daughter's primary school. I described her as a loyal, clever ginger cat, a most beautiful creature of God who died young. With the knowledge that people who had heart transplant seem to also inherit donors' memory, I declared that a corner of my heart is forever preserved for Pasha.

Since then I lost so many of my loved ones, l feel there is less of myself now with parts of me died each time too. There is not much information about how other people convey their grief and how long it lasts, but I believe mine will last forever. For me grief is like an open wound on the heart, never heals, whenever touched it will bleed. And touched it is so often, I live in the pain of missing their presence. This time my sorrow for their absence was triggered by another death that happened near home. Kemal might be sad to hear that the garden he poured his soul in to create, the one we called a heavenly sanctuary for animals was turned into a killing field overnight.

Six months after Kemal's death, we were disturbed by some unusual noises at night. The next morning, I was shocked to see our plush garden lawn strangely lost its verdure. In a sea of pale fluffy fur sweeping through the garden, I could make out the corpse of a fox. It was like watching the end of a horror movie, I had to mull on the senseless event unfolded last night. What had the poor little fox done to deserve all this cruelty? It was unfailingly a harrowing night for the doomed cub, amidst flying fur under the early summer moon. With no culprits in sight, I wept over the rigid, tiny fox's body and tried to get rid of the numerous shameless flies teeming around the corpse. A hole on the lawn gave away how the murderous foxes pinned down the unfortunate victim and his struggle of kicking (maybe also screaming) to get out of their grasp. To see a tender life cut short by other vicious members of its own kind in such a savage manner was too much for me to bear.

How I needed my loved ones to be here! I could have told them of my heartbreak and sadness, they would have comforted me and wiped away my tears. Without their support I blamed the moon keeping cover on its dark side, wondered why the stars stopped twinkling last night. I shouted for the ruthless sky to shed some rainy tears to disperse the greedy flies, I even ordered the careless wind to play a somber tune and join me to mourn for the end of another dream. After all I prayed for the innocent fox to rest in peace in a better world.

I wished to offer the fox a decent burial and finally located a suitable spot for that purpose in our garden. With quivering hands I placed the dead fox in his grave and kept asking myself why the body of the fox was so light? Why there was no blood spilled out on the grass? Unresolved heartbreak resurfaced to torment my dejected heart: a sickly cow in the farm was slaughtered, only to be found was five months pregnant. Holding the little toy-like calf's body in his hand, Father expressed his regret for not giving the calf a chance to enter the world alive. He was not aware of the pregnancy of the ailing cow, only tried to help the long suffering animal to rid her incurable disease and pain. I was thirteen then, now fifty years on holding the fox's corpse in the box, I was equally devastated by my inability to save him. Now there are three mummified animal bodies embedded in my head. More tragedies, one sealed melancholy.

It is events like these which make me miss my loved ones the most, such is the prominence of their comforting power residing in my heart. Together we faced many catastrophes, alone I am engulfed with fear and grievous tears. I suppose in my lonely existence, deep down, the many a tears I shed is about the sad way Ibrahim and Kemal left this world. I don't know if I should believe in the therapeutic power of weeping, but I don't think they will be too pleased to see me crying a river. After all the flowers in the garden don't need rejected tears to blossom, why not leave them to nurture the precious memories in my heart.

We used to have this carefree life together, until Kemal's leukemia diagnosis had interrupted the tranquility of our days. All cancers are death sentences, but Chronic Lymphocytic Leukemia sounded not so imminent as others. With a glimmer of hope that this type of cancer develops slowly, we expected medical intervention could delay the ticking time bomb from exploding for a couple years. The baffling years his cancer cells stayed dormant were gone like a flash, soon it was time for them to multiply in Kemal's body at an alarming rate. Yet his treatment not only lagged slowly behind the rapid progression of cancer but also littered with many avoidable errors and negligence. It unquestionably robbed a year or two of his life.

With the rapid decline in Kemal's health, we visited A&E frequently in the autumn chill for possible treatment or at least some pain relief. However time after time, it was always a *computer said no* situation. There was these clinical trials Kemal eagerly awaited to participate, yet the oncologist put him in the wrong age group. After wasting six futile months for trial preparations, the oncologist was in no rush to prepare Kemal for the next age-appropriate trial with an additional six months. That became Kemal's *last days to lie in wait*, since just before the second trial about to start he was diagnosed with bladder cancer and disqualified from this one too.

Kemal looked pale, languid to tell me the deep biopsy was performed under a local anesthetic. "So?" I asked apprehensively. "It hurt a lot, I could feel every scraping", Kemal complained with pain in his eyes. The torment must be excruciating for strong-willed him even to admit the hurt. Though livid I tried to convince Kemal that the suffering could soon enable the rightful treatment to rid his bladder cancer. Little did I know that the biopsy was performed while Kemal was already under palliative care. The pure recollection of letting my dying husband experience such pain to no effect is savage enough to make me weep with my still oppressed heart.

During the meeting to discuss my complaint, the oncologist apologized for their failure in communication. Though with a bland expression he also concluded that no treatment could save Kemal's life at that stage. Then what about to give Kemal a sendoff with compassion and care, not an unnecessary biopsy to torment his body and heart. Kemal left this world angrily, since the specialists he trusted all let him down. The deep sorrow displayed by his eyes in his final days has become the only memory following me around. Today, my heart is still in pieces just because I was unable to shield Kemal's suffering from agonizing hurt under causeless operation. What can be more important than letting a man with a generous heart to feel that he was also loved when all his dreams were dying!

When fortune dispenses cancer to man, everything imparts a hellish impression. But sorrow didn't blind us from the glimpse of heaven exhibited itself around us in a heartwarming way.

It was the junior doctors in the hospital who got our thumbs up, they offered the bedridden Kemal excellent care. Their actions may not have made any difference to his fate hereafter, nor could be so, but hard working doctors they truly are. We were also impressed by their professionalism and their unfailingly kind as well as considerate efforts. We further salute the dedicated nurses, they tried their best to offer the necessary comfort for all patients and did their share in easing the suffering of the patients.

Once back home, we found an army of kindest carers in the world helping me to look after bedridden Kemal. These carers were punctual, pleasant and professional during their work. I almost burst into tears when the district nurse came to our rescue as she heard that the connector of Kemal's catheter was blocked. Since then she had been coming every two days to flush the catheter. The GP came on the night we called him to inject morphine for Kemal also encouraged me to take up the task of injection from then on. Since that night I was able to alleviate his pain regularly by injecting morphine into him, and the quality of Kemal's palliative care at home was vastly improved until the day he passed away.

Deep inside, Kemal was proud of the NHS to his heart's core, still grateful for them to discover he got cancer four years before his death. But I beg to differ. Was it a privilege to know that cancer is ravaging your body while no remedy could ever be provided? I would rather live without the knowledge of it, if treatment is no more than a fantasy. The policy of *watchful waiting* and *active surveillance* is the prettier alternative spelling for waiting to die. Then living unmindfully is far more comforting than a worried existence.

In cancer, it is waste of time to address the cause and effect. It inevitably comes, tortures and kills half of our human population. It is one of those nasty surprises of life, just lurking in the corner, waiting for an opportunity to attack. Medication works for some lucky ones, when cancer cells are eradicated early enough through surgery or chemotherapy. Yes, the chemotherapy, it doesn't discriminate among good or bad cells, leaves some without cancer temporarily, leaves others with damaged organs permanently.

Strange enough, in Kemal's 49-year long medical career, he never witnessed any virus as pernicious as COVID-19. If it ever happened in his lifetime, I know how he would throw himself into the operation of saving others selflessly with healer's familiarity. He would not mind to lose his own life during the process, and could wave goodbye to me with a smile then offer me comforting words like 'everyone dies, but you still have got my soul dwelling in our house'. That, in all likelihood, would be a more fitting farewell for him.

Time hasn't dulled my pain or softened my despair from Kemal's tragic death. I struggled to bid farewell to Kemal peacefully at his deathbed for the inability to shake off the true grievances from the unfortunate medical negligence. No words could soothe his crestfallen heart as each day became more grim than the previous one, but a wonderfully moonlit night conjured up images in Kemal's head of our faraway loved ones. 'Below the same moon, we staring at the identical moonscape' he uttered in a whisper. I joined in with Li Bai's poem before Kemal's bright world went dim again after this fleeting moment. The famous Chinese poet from the Tang Dynasty initially mistook the moonlight as ground frost, but when he looked up, the sight of magnificent moonlight captivated his fancy, reminding him of his distant homeland.

Where exactly was his remembered home, Kemal asked. I like to think that Li Bai's spirit drifted to Central Asia when he wrote this poem, his sweet birth place Kyrgyzstan. Moonlight was a recurring theme in his poems, Li Bay even named his daughter Aynur, a popular Turkic name for girls. His daughter was known as Mingyue Nu among the Han Chinese. Mingyue is Chinese bright moon just as what Aynur means in our language. Literary giants don't get lost in translation. Actually Li Bai created a semantically and metaphorically enriched brand new name with an additional word Nu, which means slave befittingly but aurally sounds like the last syllable in Aynur. With such an exotic name, the daughter of the famous poet was mythically known as the *slave of the alluring moon* by ordinary folks who had no knowledge about the origin of the moniker.

A great part of Li Bai's poetries are about the places he visited and friends he saw on the way. He enjoyed his long wandering journey and recorded many stages of his travels with detailed and vivid descriptions. His characterization of nature is impressive and historic, reflects his ingenious observations and unmatched imagination. The loneliness he felt in remote lands did not make Li Bai more reticent but nonetheless determined to explore the power of prolific life that suited his adventurous ego. Kemal was fascinated by the celestial beauty of shamanic overture in Li Bay's poetry. An influence decidedly from sky-worshiping Kyrgyz.

Travelling is a luxury, even more so if one strolls around purposefully to discover the dust of our form. With hearts fond of exploration, our adventurous forefathers were never put off by the rough roads ahead. They sang the folk songs while watching the eagles beating their wings to reach the frosty sky; they recorded the very pretty blossom along the valleys with stream to flow by; they crossed the endless grassland and stood on the peaky mountain to watch the sun rise. The spheres of their journey enabled them to dive into a brand new culture and live through it in the nomadic empire they created.

As their descendants, we must have inherited their itinerant hearts and made travelling a big part of our lives. Oh yes, we traveled a lot. My long train journey started at the age of 14 and it was an expedition along the entire length of the Great Wall of China. To be precise, I entered Shanhaiguan[3] from the east 18 hours after I boarded the train from Harbin, then came out from the west pass four days later, still on the train. The Jade Gate was not the least as spectacular as the Shanhaiguan, not even a shade of emerald can be seen as the name indicated. To clear my dazed mind I asked the Han Chinese sitting next to me about the jade; with a cheerful grin he pointed to the direction where the train was heading. Besides oil and minerals I then became aware of the tangible existence of jade in our expansive desert. No wonder railways were built up to here in a hurry, as reflected by a Chinese saying that *when the train rings, gold is worth a thousand taels.*

The Great Wall was a fortification to keep Uyghurs, Tibetans and Mongolians away from the heartland of China. Actually to keep the Manchurians at bay too, until one of the Qing Emperors was so enthralled by Mandarin, he even ordered the completion of a Chinese dictionary consisting of no less than 47,000 entries. With the Yuan Dynasty together, foreign forces had controlled China for more than 300 years. There is no reason that why China shouldn't take the occupations in their stride, not least of which because it gave them the opportunity to assimilate the Manchurians entirely. The Great Wall has never deterred the Han Chinese economic migrants to end up in Central Asia. The migrants might be impelled to leave their home by poverty, but justified their arrival with the excuse to gentrify our area. It is our modern day refugees that gets my true sympathy, who are leaving the charming olive groves, Assyrian gardens, blue skies and full-blazing sun behind just to escape war and prosecution.

As always Kemal returned to his egalitarian ideology that the resources should be shared equally by all citizens of our planet. The communist Chinese did start their governance just like that and it turned out to be the beginning of its darkest hours, with brutal capital punishment for many innocent landowners. The impoverished peasants were encouraged to retell their sordid past in the rally, until the mass was reduced into collective sobbing. The hysteria would lead to some so-called victims leaping up on the stage to violently attack the already handcuffed landlords. Often the emotions would run so high, some unfortunate landowners were even executed on the spot, just based on the flimsy evidence from few self pitying individuals who couldn't get over their sorrowful past. The landowners were never given a chance to challenge the neurotic accusers' version of *truth* before swiftly being shot by the senseless fire squads on basic impulse.

If taking away the land from landowners could be justified, then distributing the household possessions of one rich family to the entire village was nothing short of ridiculous and futile. Actually the fraught silence of the wealthy minority was never the concern of the state, the focus was on the large number of proletariats. Many a books were written about owning a used quilt, bedsheet or a pillow by the mass as a worthy acquisition. The narrative about a young woman excitedly took up an embroidered pillow for her upcoming nuptial almost got teenage me chocked on breakfast marmalade. One pillow for wedding, she needed at least two! The propaganda about the sharing of goods more or less openly claimed that human race is fueled by the desire to be equally poor.

However the euphoria of owning a piece of land was short lived for farmers, since the Communist government never exactly fancied landowners, let alone to face so many of them. Sadly working for the unresponsive People's Commune turned out to be much worse than working for the *ox-ghost and serpent-spirited* landlords, since the grains were distributed by consumption rather than contribution at the end of the year. The commune members were ordered to be submissive and grateful to the state even without the promised radical improvement in their lives. No one bothered about poor harvest until the arrival of the inevitable famine. Though the farmers were worse off but they were relieved to know that communism was only about sharing land, not their wives as rumour had it.

With a non-refined ideology, communism ruled under division and disparity. Instead of a harmonious society, we were engulfed by the darkness of class warfare. Whichever way you turn, you gaze at frustration or confrontation. Even in primary school children lived retrospectively by getting to know each other's ancestors. The poorer down your family-tree line the more equality you would get, as if the communism came to existence to change the fortunes or deliver karma for a few. My grandfathers could never have known that the end result of their hard work could have inflicted serious harm on the career of their offspring half a century later.

Luckily Father was able to present himself as a

middle class farmer's son, as his early life of comfort thousands of miles away was safely his own knowledge. Not realising that Father was trying to convince the authority and protect us at the same time, I envied the privileges enjoyed by those poor peasants' offspring. The only consolation for me came from the feudal sexism, my maternal grandfather's businessman status was more of my aunt's problem rather than mine. It ended my very bright aunt's academic dream. University degrees were like gold dust at those days, mainly because baby boomers outnumbered the university's places by almost a thousand to one. As a result the state made the class system discernible by eliminating those young applicants with parents who were wealthy once upon a time.

Chuchai was an official holiday. It was customary to see the communist members to disappear for a few weeks and come back with a healthy glow. I asked someone what she did during *Chuchai*, she told me it was about to find out a colleague's true background. Of course living in a five star hotel with banquets on a daily basis. It must be another refugee from a far away province, claiming to be the son of a poor peasant. The first-hand evidence could be used to persecute the man for his lies. From 1949 onward, the Chinese communist government spent billions of yuan to *dig out others' dirt*. I believe Father could have been investigated if he had pretended that my grandfather was a poor peasant before *liberation* (that is what communist took over from 1949 was called).

The privileged life higher ranked government officials lived only became clear to the great public during the Cultural Revolution. We ordinary folks were given a glance of their luxury lives while they were stripped from their positions temporarily (once Cultural Revolution was over, the survivors were paid back many folds over). Once I joined the queue to visit an exhibition centre, formerly the home of the governor for Heilongjiang province. Within ten minutes' walk from where we lived, he resided in many rooms, manicured lawn clearly taken care by gardener which reminded me of the one described in the *Red Chambers Dream*.

My friend felt sorry that I missed the best display there, the room with hundreds of pairs of shoes and clothes belonging to the punished official's wife and daughters. A few years later, one famous Uyghur dancer recalled her ordeal during cultural revolutionary time. She secretly got out from her captive one day in disguise just to visit her own home curiously. She was shocked to see so many goods displayed in her house, but she claimed that not all the possessions on parade belonged to herself. A lot of the clothes and shoes were added by the Red Guards to make her look corrupt with venal extravaganza.

Actually the true exposure of the communist

leader' lavish lifestyles became public knowledge after Lin Biao[4] was killed in the plane crash. To turn the public against him as someone plotted to murder and replace the supreme Chairman Mao, his son's decadent lifestyle was leaked to the general public. According to the anecdote, Lin Liguo brought hundreds of girls from all corners of China to choose his ideal bride. Some pretty girls were kidnapped for being unwilling to go. Once the girls were in his residence, he would watch them naked having showers from his secret camera with his trusted friends in company.

Three young Uyghur beauties were also brought in to be his bride candidates just before Lin Liguo perished together with his parents. The authorities tried to send the girls back to where they were picked up, but they refused. The girls didn't have a clue they were in Beijing for display, they were brought in with the promise of some prestigious jobs. They were the envy of everyone as they started their journey and now they wanted Beijing to deliver it. To get rid of these three trouble makers, Chinese authorities sent them to university to study. I know at least one of them completed her degree successfully and has become a medical doctor, a very pretty doctor indeed.

The communist ideology even failed to gain a devoted mass following in China, but the authorities imposed Marxism, Leninism and Chairman Mao's thoughts on us just the same.

These people with their paramount importance are the undisputable icons and role models for each of us. Their lifestyle, likes and dislikes are used to shape our habits. The greatest philosopher is Hegel we were told, since Karl Marx liked his idea. The greatest writer is Maxim Gorky, since he was Stalin's favourite. There is this painting where Gorky reading to smiling Stalin and few other top rank Soviet leaders figuratively. In reality there was never such a moment in the history: the two men, Stalin and Gorky, couldn't stand each other. But Stalin did promote Gorky, since his autobiographical books about his childhood painted a gloomy and poverty-stricken picture of the pre communist era in Russia.

No one is denying that people did live improvised lives all over the world more than a century ago. The suffering in Charles Dickens' *Great Expectations* as well as *Les Miserables* from Victor Hugo were all too real. However the misery is now largely a thing of the past in the West with the arrival of new technologies combined with the discovery of fossil energy. Society produced wealth instead of sharing existing pieces, finally there were plenty of jobs to employ everyone. Those unable to work can also survive comfortably with the help of the state. A welfare society era is born, but in the West only.

As children under communist regimes we were brought up to believe that there was not even a sunny day in the *old society*. The films about life before the communist era were always dark accompanied with ominous sound of music, then something suddenly goes wrong in our hero's life. There was this film from North Korea about the fate of twin girls. The one who remained with father in South Korea ended up becoming a bar maid after father died in a road traffic accident. The lucky one was smuggled to North Korea and adopted by music professors to become a famous dancer. Confused children couldn't tell the difference between the personal tragedy and the unfairness of the society. All they knew was that nobody smiled until the communists brought in sunshine, laughter, food and shelter.

In the early 1950s, an impoverished Uyghur man was so delighted by the downfall of his landlord he decided to go to Beijing to thank Chairman Mao, riding a donkey he finally owned. Kurban Tulum might not have any idea what a tough and long journey he embarked on, but seeing many people went to Mecca and made it back probably inspired him just to carry a few extra tandoori bread as precaution. Besides, the claim that all roads lead to the magnificent Beijing by broadcast could have boosted his undaunted spirit. Though he didn't manage to go beyond Urumqi, his determination and desire impressed the Chinese authorities, as a result he was taken to Beijing by train and received by Chairman Mao in 1958. He became a symbol of national unity with a photo of him shaking hands with Mao splashed all over the country's press.

Chairman Mao's gaze usually revealed a lot about his inner thoughts when he met with others. With fascination Mao stared at Che Guevara admiringly, as if trying to work out why this young, dashing and courageous warrior had joined his communist camp. However in this circumstance Kurban Tulum was bestowed by Mao, but Mao was certainly bemused by his bare-chested look. Under Kurban Tulum's petticoat, which is called *chapan* in Uyghur, he had neither vest nor shirt to cover his torso. Was it the authorities' deliberate anti-lavish makeover or just Kurban Tulum's eccentric fashion sense? Father wasn't a fan, wouldn't even bother to answer.

The statue of Kurban Tulum shaking hands with Mao is standing in Khotan Unity Square, and his descendants were invited to Beijing for a follow-up documentary recently. While he certainly managed to flip his fortune from the bottom to the top of the society, it wasn't uncommon to see people hungry and unable to afford underwear decades after the communist reign. In the 1980s, with Chairman Mao safely dead, thus unable to insist *four legs good*, China finally joined the *two-legged* global technological race. This has transformed China into the global manufacturing powerhouse, which created many billionaires instead of spreading wealth and still without social welfare. The single-minded economical pursuit also has detrimental ecological consequences. The author of *Wolf Totem* admitted that relatives from Mongolia felt no envy for the poor grassland and declining wolf populations from their wealthier Inner Mongolian relatives. Adaptive wolves have wasted no time to emigrate to the ecologically sound Mongolia for their survival and howling on their steppe to the local's pride.

The wealthy China is less equal than ever while the world now has an unbridgeable gap between the wealthy North and Global South. Even more so than the time John Lennon *Imagined* that harmony could be easily enacted one day. What would Kemal say if he sees our vaccine inequality during COVID-19 vaccine era? I could picture him turning inside his grave with his forever medically caring heart. Kemal sounded his alarm of the possibility that the technological race might shatter our fragile world peace one day. In his poem *Guardians of the Peace* he declared *In the name of God/In the name of colour/Since the time of Cain/We are killing each other.* He didn't live long enough to fear about the Russia and Ukraine conflict turning into nuclear warfare, but did spend nine days anxiously worried how the Cuban Crisis would unfold. However Kemal's answer to stop the world spinning out of control in the wrong direction is that we become *guardians of peace/soldiers of justice* and treat the *world as our temple/science as our prophet.*

Being one of the millions of doctors in the world hardly qualifies Kemal to be remembered as someone who made history. After all what is history? Is it about those who are still relevant after death? Then Kemal certainly earned his stripes within the family history. We haven't stopped thinking and talking about him since he left. In all likelihood Kemal's patients may also fondly remember his dedication, especially at moments of need for good doctors or after an unsatisfactory medical intervention.

Remembering Kemal's wisdom has a healing power to my heart, I have become aware of the fact that we mortals still have a chance to carry on fighting for a better world ahead. With all the sadness around us it's not about to stay *comfortably numb* but to use our voice to influence our future towards a brighter direction. I don't let tears cloud my eyes any more even when the golden morning sunshine spoils my joy by letting the radiant light fall on Kemal's empty seat. It is a desolate house without him, but carrying out my duty to his wishes keeps my heart full and chases away the gloom. No breakfast together, no news discussion, no Kemal telling me about his thought-provoking worldview. However his insight is here to stay and to enrich my life.

Many summer evenings before bedtime I sit quietly in the garden to indulge in vivid memory of my once upon a time less troubled life. When I look around for the view of my loved ones' existence under dreamy sky, I do feel their divine influence. My solace comes from enduringly smooth and velvety lawn, from the two oleanders which dwarf other plants with their height and continue to blossom opulently throughout summer. There are more camellias now, but none can rival the striking vision of that tall, red, thirty-year-old tree. Its luscious, bushy, glossy leaves act like a veil for birds to hide from our view and chirp all day. I often happily dwell in the garden, listening to the music from birds then walk into the celestial world to discuss birds' melodious orchestra with my loved ones there while the live performance unfolds.

The other day Kemal's sister worried about her inability to locate him among the sizzling stars in the shiny sky. I would rather look for him in the perceivable realm such as the *gentle autumn rain, glowing ocean waves* or the soft evening breeze. How we all people live under the anesthetic effect of afterlife metaphors. Closer to home I see him, the invisible constant gardener tidying the elegantly hanging bushy ivy or trimming the stunning garden rose named *Lightning Strike.* His starring role is tinting my life with a pink shaded fusion of the past, the present and maybe the future too.

There are still times I wish there is no sorrow that the memory of my loved ones' laughter can't heal, and I should be satisfied while counting the blessings of the delight they had brought me to feel. Father considered those who couldn't forgive and forget as the weaker species, but with all the burdens of guilt, it is hard to be strong and free. We who lost loved ones live guiltily ever after. I wish I spent more time with Father, Mother and Ibrahim in their heydays and just simply joined Kemal every time when he eagerly invited me for tea in the garden shade. Yearning for my loss provides me nostalgia to lament the death and as a consequence the vanished past.

Of all the departed souls around me it is Father's mentor Memtili Efendi's demise I mourn the most. I always have this image of the 36-year-old him in that unreachable moment: looking out of the prison barred window then engulfed by infernal blaze which burned him into charcoal. He was not identified with his DNA or dental record in the skeletal prison pared by fire, maybe nobody was in Central Asia at that time. It was the pair of boots he newly bought on his feet which garnered attention in the twilight. In a planet only preoccupied with the world wars, we were wholly unknown and left out from the inking of the history. But we were also frozen, burned, shot and bombed to death ruthlessly during our struggle for freedom.

Memtili Efendi's body was secretly taken back to Atush and could only be buried in an unidentified grave. Often a dim emptiness spread over my heart when I remember there not even a gravestone was allowed for him. What was in his mind when the flames approached him? He wasn't the type of man to complain about the remote and hard-to-attain happiness, it must be his unfulfilled ambition to educate the next generation of Uyghur youth that saddened him. A life that was born great and dedicated to helping the others to achieve greatness would have never been cut short if we Uyghurs had some sort of control of our destiny. His sacrifice springs eternity for his phenomenal legacy and continually opening up many Uyghurs' hearts and minds to let in the knowledge.

For Memtili Efendi the best music emerges from the nation that experienced the most human suffering, that probably explains our obsession with singing and dancing. With hopeful lyrics and melody arising within us, Uyghur music can carry us lightly to where we prefer to be. It enables us to look back at our past without bitterness and stare at our future with smiles as well as our transcendental musical comprehension.

NOTES

1. Xinjiang officially became a province of China in 1857 during the time of the Qing Dynasty. Since then the Qing and subsequent Nationalist Government of China had been sending governors to rule the area. In 1930s, Jiang Kaishi's government appointed Sheng Shicai, a ruthless Han Chinese warlord, as the governor to comply with their traditional policy to 'let the barbarians to fight it out among themselves'. To achieve an absolute control in the far west away from his bosses, Sheng Shicai pretended to be a communist and gained Stalin's complete support with his Nationalist authorities' silent approval. They even left him to deal with his budget deficit savagely as Sheng took up Stalin's advice to plant crimes on a vast number of wealthy Uyghurs and confiscated their wealth after their execution. The bloodshed and sheer terror he created was unprecedented in Uyghur history. During The Second World War, when Stalin was busy fighting Germans, Sheng denounced his communist faith

and rejoined the Chinese Nationalist party. He was replaced by another Han Chinese governor until the People's Liberation Army marched into Xinjiang. Sheng Shicai escaped to Taiwan in 1949 with Jiang Kaishi and lived the rest of his life there.

2. *The Dream of the Red Chamber* is one of the four great classical novels from Chinese literature and my true favourite. The story in the book (also called *The Story of Stone*) is complex, fascinating and subsequently reveals the worldview and lifestyle of people who lived in 18th century China. The best developed male character in the book is the protagonist Bao Yu, the precious stone turned human being who came to experience the joy and sorrow in the *Red Dust* (our earthly life on this planet). He was a true feminist like no other. He threw himself on the make-up corner as an infant and ignored the books and pens on the other side, which could have predicted a successful cleric career for his future. He also claimed 'girls are made of water while men are like clay', that was why he felt purified and invigorated in the presence of girls and felt contaminated as well as oppressed when men were around. After reading the book many times, all that remains in my mind is Bao Yu and the influence of many other distinctive female characters around him.

There is the wise and all-powerful Matriarch, who doted on Bao Yu so he could spend all his days with girls but not books; the sharp-witted and resourceful Phoenix, who ran the household with an iron fist and knew everything going on in the mansions more than all the men put together; the romantic and tragic Black Jade, who was Bao Yu's childhood sweetheart then died of the grief as they couldn't marry each other; the sensible and tactful Precious Virtues who Bao Yu had to marry at last and was left pregnant on her own when Bao Yu was taken back to the Dome of Heaven.

3. Shanhaiguan is the starting point of the east entrance to the Great Wall of China. It was built as the defensive outpost against Manchurian invasion. Yumenguan (Jade Gate) is the westernmost post from the Great Wall. The gate has such a bejeweled name because of the many jade caravans that traveled through it from Khotan.

4. Lin Biao was always Mao's confidant and his preferred successor. In 1930, when the communist China opened up a military college, Mao fondly called Lin Biao the only person in entire China fit to be the Dean for that college, whereas Stalin considered Lin as a genius based on his military operations. After 1949

Mao became the head of the communist party as well as the top leader for the Chinese People's Liberation Army. Lin Biao commanded the army too but was lower in rank. It wasn't hard for Mao to secure Lin Biao's support to start The Cultural Revolution in exchange for Lin's full control of the army, but they fell out after a couple of years. The official version was that Lin Biao tried to assassinate Mao with the intention to replace him as the supreme leader, it was hard to see the logic behind it. As the younger one between the two, Lin was bound to become the leader of China once Mao died, but I guess the 'gang of four' had other plans. Despite us being obliged to spend years to daily chanting of 'long live Chairman Mao ('ten thousand years for Chairman Mao' in Chinese), then followed by 'forever healthy wishes for vice Chairman Lin', he was made to flee with his wife and son for reasons only they knew. The plane crashed in outer Mongolia as it ran out of fuel. The teacher told us that Lin was aiming to reach Soviet Union to continue his anti-revolutionary activities. Chairman Mao and revolution were used interchangeably during my school days.

PHOTOGRAPHS

Figure 1: Ehmetjan Qasimi, president of East Turkestan Republic between 1944 to 1947. He was 35 when he died in the plane crash.

*Figure 2: Memtili Efendi, the eminent Uyghur scholar
and inspirational educator in 1930s.
(courtesy to Mirehmet Siyip, Yalkun Ruzi and
Ablekim Zordun from: Memtili Efendi)*

Figure 3: My 35-year old father, Mehmet Ibrahim Aji.

Figure 4: My 28-year old mother, Amine Imin Aji.

Figure 5: My 20-year-old brother Ibrahim as I remember him.

Figure 6: Heliqe, my 25-year-old sister-in-law.

Figure 7: My husband Kemal in his GP surgery.

Figure 8: My hero uncle who saved his neighbour, Ablemit Imin Aji

Figure 9: Kurban Tulum meets Chairman Mao in 1958.

Figure 10: Chairman Mao and Che Guevara in 1960 (courtesy to Jung Chang from Mao: The Unknown Story).

Figure 11: Front and back views of a duttar
Jo Dusepo, CC BY-SA 4.0, via Wikimedia Commons

Figure 12: Morin hkuur, a Mongolian stringed instrument
Michael Coghlan from Adelaide, Australia, CC BY-
SA 2.0, via Wikimedia Commons

Figure 13: The eastern entrance to the Great Wall

BenBenW, CC BY 2.0, via Wikimedia Commons

Figure 14: The western exit of the Great Wall. This is the real Jade Gate

John Hill, CC BY-SA 3.0, via Wikimedia Commons

ACKNOWLEDGEMENTS

I feel extremely grateful to my parents for keeping Uyghur history and culture alive with storytelling and singing during my formative years. When I was teaching in Xinjiang Technological College, my students all enthusiastically joined me in discussions of the authenticity about my parents' oral citations.

My heartfelt thanks go to Mirehmet Siyip, Yalkun Ruzi and Ablekim Zordun for courageously publishing the book Memtili Efendi, which is filled with valuable information missing from my father's narrative. Their book was timely written in the late 1990s when many relations and students of Memtili Efendi were still alive. It is like a mini encyclopaedia of the turbulent Uyghur existence in the 1930s. I am also in awe of those grief-stricken relatives of Memtili Efendi, while taking care of his charred body they also tried their best to memorize all the poems he inscribed on the prison wall.

Last but not least I want to thank my elder daughter, Bella, for being the first reader, the spontaneous editor and candid critic of my entire work. Now, looking back, I can see that without all these amazing people mentioned earlier, the publication of this book would not have been possible.

ABOUT THE AUTHOR

Melike

The author Melike was born in Ghulja, Xinjiang. After travelling the whole length of China, she emigrated to the Far East with her parents at the age of two. She went to study in Harbin Engineering University then returned to teach in Xinjiang Technological College upon graduation. In 1984, she obtained a scholarship from the British Council to study in Imperial College. She lives in London with her disabled daughter.

Twitter: @MelikeEcin

Printed in Great Britain
by Amazon

25851558R00096